GW00684964

TIBETAN GRAMMAR: THE APPLICATION OF GENDER SIGNS CLARIFIED

ADVANCED TIBETAN GRAMMARS BY YANGCHEN DRUBPAY DORJE

TONY DUFF

PADMA KARPO TRANSLATION COMMITTEE

Copyright © 2009 Tony Duff. All rights reserved. No portion of this book may be reproduced in any form or by any means, electronic or mechanical, including photography, recording, or by any information storage or retrieval system or technologies now known or later developed, without permission in writing from the publisher.

First edition, August 2009
Second edition, March 2019
ISBN: paper book 978-9937-572-28-6
ISBN: e-book 978-9937-572-27-9

Janson typeface with diacritical marks and
Tibetan Classic Chogyal typeface
Designed and created by Tony Duff

Produced, Printed, and Published by
Padma Karpo Translation Committee
Ely, Minnesota 55731
U.S.A.

Committee members for this book: translation and composition, Tony Duff; editorial assistance, Sandy Hinzelin; cover design, Christopher Duff.

Web-site and e-mail contact through:
http://www.pktc.org/pktc
https://www.pktcshop.com
or search Padma Karpo Translation Committee on the web.

CONTENTS

INTRODUCTION

1. The Native Texts of Tibetan Grammar

According to Tibetan history, Thumi Saṃbhoṭa[1] defined the grammar of Tibetan language early in the 7th century C.E. in a series of eight very compact treatises. In the centuries after that until now, a number of scholars in Tibet have written commentaries to explain the meaning of the treatises. For Tibetan culture, these two types of texts—the defining treatises and the commentaries on them—are the fundamental texts through which Tibetan grammar is correctly known.

Basic Tibetan grammar is not too difficult to learn. However, to master all of it, including what are known as "the difficult points" of the grammar, is difficult. And for someone to master all of it to the point that he could write an authentic commentary on Thumi's defining treatises is very difficult. Thus, despite the fourteen centuries that have elapsed from Thumi's time until

---

[1] Thumi Saṃbhoṭa had several names, including the "Thonmi Saṃbhoṭa" that has become popular in recent times. Thumi is his actual name; Thonmi refers to his village.

now, there have not been many commentaries written to explain his defining treatises. And then, of the ones that have been written, only a few have gained sufficient respect that they have achieved widespread use as fundamental texts for studying grammar.

The commentaries which are most widely used for the study of Tibetan grammar today were written in the eighteenth and nineteenth centuries C.E. during a time of renaissance in learning and practice in Tibet. To begin with, the eighth Situ of the Karma Kagyu lineage of Tibetan Buddhism, a man of extraordinary learning and realization, wrote a grand commentary on grammar that re-vitalized the understanding of grammar throughout Tibet. Following that, other authors wrote a number of commentaries which agreed with and re-stated the understanding expressed in Situ's commentary, notably the Gelugpa masters Ngulchu Dharmabhadra and Yangchen Drubpay Dorje.

2. The Need to Study Tibetan Grammar Using Native Texts

When studying the grammar of a country's language, it is usual to rely on the grammar texts of that language. Therefore, it is reasonable to expect that the fundamental texts of Tibetan grammar outlined above would be the basis that non-Tibetans would use in studying the grammar of Tibetan language. However, and rather strangely, that has not been the case. Instead, some westerners have written books—primarily in English, French, and German languages—according to their idea of Tibetan grammar and these have become the books used for the purpose, even though their books do not follow Tibetan grammar as it is understood by Tibetans, but versions that only approximate it at best.

One of the biggest problems with these books is that what they present as Tibetan grammar is not actual Tibetan grammar as understood by Tibetans but a version of it which has been developed empirically. That is to say, the western authors involved have learned Tibetan grammar by observing Tibetan texts and deducing from that what the rules of Tibetan grammar must be. I was there when that approach first appeared in the early 1970's when Tibetan Buddhism and Tibetan language were first coming to the West. Almost no references to the language were in print and our knowledge of the Tibetan language was not sufficient to understand Tibetan grammar texts, so we had little choice but to take this empirical approach to understanding the grammar. However, these empirically-derived books about Tibetan grammar are now outmoded and really must be rejected as unsuited to the task. The time has arrived when we should learn the details of Tibetan grammar as it actually is and should be using the native texts of Tibetan grammar to do that.

Another major problem is that some of these books by westerners loudly proclaim systems for understanding Tibetan grammar which have no relationship at all to the systems of native Tibetan grammar. An outstanding example is the "science of the dots", which is loudly proclaimed in a major publication from western university-based scholars called as the basis for parsing and hence understanding written Tibetan language. The principal author, a friend of mine, defended his work to me by saying that his approach was found to be helpful in teaching Tibetan grammar to American students. I drily replied that his complicated system, which has nothing at all to do with native Tibetan grammar, has held back students because of filling their heads with strange ideas about it. In fact, I have found that teaching students the actual system of parsing Tibetan text as it appears in Tibetan grammar is easier than teaching them his invented system and certainly allows them to understand Tibetan language more quickly. This is not speculation; I have seen it to be so in grammar classes I have taught where I have had to patiently undo the strange system of the "science of the dots" that the students had learned from the book mentioned just above. Once the students were taught the fundamentals of the native grammar of Tibet and how they are to be applied to the process of parsing Tibetan text, they were relieved and reported that knowing the actual Tibetan system of grammar was vastly superior to knowing the system of the dots and other such inventions. I have also found that students who learned the various empirically-derived understandings of Tibetan grammar referred to above are relieved when they find out how Tibetan grammar actually works and universally report that their ability to understand the language has improved by leaps and bounds.

In spite of the fact that these books do not represent and more often than not mis-represent Tibetan grammar, they have become the basis for teaching Tibetan language and its grammar around the world: in the study programs for foreigners given at Tibetan Buddhist monasteries and the like in Nepal, India, and so on; in western university degree courses; in western Dharma centres where Tibetan language is taught; and so on. Because of them the basics of Tibetan language and its grammar have almost universally been mis-taught and mis-learned amongst non-Tibetans. Especially, their use has resulted in western translators of Tibetan Buddhism who do not really understand the grammar of the Tibetan language and whose translations suffer as a result.

As an example of this problem, some years ago Bengchen Tenga Rinpoche gave his annual course for westerners at his monastery in Nepal. He taught a text on Mahamudra that presented Mahamudra in a series of verses that were brilliantly composed with the very clever use of Tibetan grammar. Tenga Rinpoche's translator simply could not translate the material because he only knew Tibetan grammar from these empirically-derived works on Tibetan grammar that have been written by westerners. The translator was simply at a loss. His oral translation did not present the meaning of the text and teaching that went with it and, after the week of teaching had ended, none of the students got any of the meaning that Tenga Rinpoche was trying to get across to them. The teaching failed not because of the teacher, but because of a translator who simply did not understand Tibetan grammar as Tibetans understand it. Afterwards, I translated some of the text for some students who had stayed on in Nepal for a while. They were astounded at what they had missed out on. Such a sad story! Unfortunately, I have many others like it.

It is universally understood in the general world of translating and interpreting that a person who is going to translate matters of importance into another language first needs a good and correct understanding of his own language and then needs the same for the target language. In my own, direct experience, far too many people who call themselves Tibetan translators do not even know the grammar of their own language, let alone that of Tibetan. A significant factor in their not fully understanding Tibetan grammar is the books and teaching systems mentioned above that present a modified version of what Tibetan grammar actually is.

All in all, there is an outstanding need for books in languages other than Tibetan which show Tibetan grammar as it actually is. There is also an outstanding need to realize that the translation of Tibetan texts has to be based on a proper understanding of their grammar as defined in native Tibetan grammar texts.

3. A Set of Books to Fulfil that Need

In order to fulfil this need for Tibetan grammar texts that could be used as a basis for studying Tibetan grammar on its own terms, I undertook the major work of making a set of publications that would include Thumi's defining treatises and a number of respected commentaries to them, together with the explanations that would, for the first time, present Tibetan grammar to non-Tibetans in an authentic way. My aspiration for the work was that the books in general would have a very positive effect on the work of translating Tibetan Buddhist texts into other languages and in particular would result in a much higher level of quality and accuracy in the translations.

To do this work, I first had to became familiar with Thumi's defining treatises and also with the various commentaries to them, both old and new. I accomplished this through intensive studies done in the 1990's in India and Nepal with the most highly regarded Tibetan grammarians of the time. It is noteworthy that I did these studies in purely Tibetan environments, with no special arrangement made for non-Tibetans. My spoken Tibetan was already very good from years of living with Tibetans and doing oral translation for various Tibetan teachers, and I used this to advantage, learning the grammar entirely from Tibetans in Tibetan language in a purely Tibetan environment. My studies included a three month course of explanations of the entire great commentary by the eighth Situ given at the Tibetan Institute for Higher Studies in Sarnath, northern India.

In light of the knowledge of Tibetan grammatical literature gained during those studies, it seemed that the best commentaries to make available would be the ones most highly regarded and hence most used amongst Tibetans nowadays, that is, the commentaries which express Tibetan grammar as the eighth Situ explained it. My principal grammar teacher, the late Padma Gyaltsen of the Tibetan Institute of Higher Studies—who was regarded as the very best of Tibetan grammarians of his time and who certainly knew the details of the entire range of grammar commentaries that had ever been written in Tibet—agreed.

Therefore, I worked for several years on a set of books that would present the most important native Tibetan grammar texts in translation and, moreover, with all the background, glossaries, vocabulary, and so on needed to make the grammar of Tibet as Tibetans understand it not only readily comprehensible by Westerners but useful to them in a practical way.

Briefly stated, the set of books consists of two standard references to Tibetan grammar—one for each of the two extant treatises of Thumi Saṃbhoṭa—and four books each containing a specific commentary to those treatises, with the commentaries being the most popular ones in use today, commentaries which follow Situ's great commentary.[2]

---

[2] These titles are available through the PKTC web-site and shop, whose internet addresses are given on the copyright page.

The two standard references explain every detail of the grammar in a gradual way that allows beginners and scholars alike complete access to the grammar. Unlike most Western books on Tibetan grammar, the explanations included present Tibetan grammar as Tibetans understand it, though they are written so that any Westerner can easily understand them.

The first standard reference deals with history, lineages of grammar, and all the other background information needed to have a good feel for Tibetan grammar. It continues with a long presentation of the meaning of the primary text that defines Tibetan grammar, Thumi Saṃbhoṭa's treatise called *The Root of Grammar, The Thirty Verses*. This standard reference as I have called it is a very large work, containing an enormous level of detail of all relevant aspects of Tibetan grammar, and with very extensive yet easy-to-comprehend explanations of these points of grammar that show the actual Tibetan grammar in a way that works for Western minds. Step by step the explanations build a complete picture of the language and, as they do so, of all the grammar terminology involved. The standard reference faithfully presents Tibetan grammar as Tibetans understand it and as it must be understood by anyone involved with Tibetan translation. However, it includes extensive explanations which make that Tibetan understanding both comprehensible and immediately useful to Westerners because it allows them to connect that understanding with English grammar at least.

The second standard reference is written in the same detailed yet immediately useful way as the first volume. However, it deals with the subject matter of the other, remaining treatise on Tibetan grammar called *The Application of Gender Signs*. This standard reference is shorter than the first because it does not contain the extensive presentation of background material found in the first volume and because the subject matter of the second volume can be dealt with in fewer words, even though it is technically much more difficult. It is noteworthy that it includes the first complete and correct treatment of the theory of verbs and transitive-intransitive verbal actions seen in English, a topic which has confused most people because of its complexity and the absence of proper, Tibetan-grammar-based explanations of it.

The commentaries selected as supports for the explanations of the defining treatises in the two standard references to Tibetan grammar follow the eighth Situ's commentaries. They are:

- The two *Great Living Tree* grammars by Yangchen Drub pay Dorje which are the subject of this book;
- *Situ's Words* by Ngulchu Dharmabhadra;
- *The Essence of the Elegant Thorough Explanation* by Khenpo Ngedon Jamyang;
- Two commentaries to *The Application of Gender Signs* by Yangchen Drubpay Dorje.

The first standard reference also has a long chapter on pronunciation, revealing details of correct Tibetan pronunciation that still have not been seen in English. To go with that, there is a text on pronunciation by Sonam Tsemo, an early master of the Sakya tradition.

This introduction goes on to expand on the information given just above. First it gives information on Thumi's defining treatises, then on each of the commentarial texts, and finally still more information on the *Great Living Tree* grammars by Yangchen Drubpay Dorje which are the subject of this book. If you would like to see even more detailed information on all of this, together with extensive presentations of the history and lineages of Tibetan grammar, please read the first standard reference mentioned just above.

4. Thumi's Treatises that Define Tibetan Grammar

In the seventh century C.E., the Tibetan man Thumi Saṃbhoṭa wrote eight treatises[3] which defined the lettering set and grammar for Tibetan language. They are the original treatises defining the Tibetan language. The first and sixth ones are still available to us but the remaining six were lost totally and irretrievably during the ninth century C.E. purges of King Langdarma. Despite many efforts since that time by great scholars of Tibet and other countries, too, no trace of them has been found.

The first treatise of Thumi is titled *The Root of Grammar*, *"The Thirty (Verses)"*[4]. This is usually abbreviated in Tibetan to སུམ་ཅུ་པ་ or even just སུམ་ both meaning *The Thirty*[5]. The treatise is the beginning of Thumi's definition of the Tibetan language.

---

[3] Thumi referred to them as treatises (śhāstras) because that is the Indian name for a treatise that establishes or maintains a system of thought.

[4] Tib. ལུང་སྟོན་པ་རྩ་བ་སུམ་ཅུ་པ་ཞེས་བྱ་བ་, lung ston pa rtsa ba sum cu pa zhes bya ba. Tibetan, as with English has a set of irregular spellings of numbers as one proceeds through increasingly higher numerals and the spelling of སུམ་ཅུ་ for thirty is correct.

[5] Since the number thirty refers to the number of four line verses in it, the name is often translated as *The Thirty Verses* but Thumi did not add the word for verses to the title, he simply called it *The Thirty*.

Accordingly, the main part starts with a definition of the lettering set. It then defines those letters to be of three main types when building words—prefixes, name-bases, and suffixes. The rest of it then shows how the suffix letters are used to build the necessary linking elements of the language. In doing so, it mentions many other points of Tibetan grammar by name but does not define or discuss their implications. It concludes with important definitions and advice, including how to learn and use the new grammar. Overall it makes the point that knowing the suffixes and the phrase linkers is key to understanding and being proficient with the language.

The sixth treatise has the title *Grammar, The Application of Gender Signs*. The name is usually abbreviated to *Application of Gender Signs*[6] or just *Gender Signs*[7]. It would be easy to mistake this as meaning "Grammar, the entrance or guide to signs". However, Situ Chokyi Jungney and other great grammarians point out that the meaning of « འཇུག་པ་, 'jug pa » in the title is "application of" rather than "entrance to" or "guide to".

Briefly stated, *Application of Gender Signs* defines a system of gender for the letters of the Tibetan alphabet and shows how the system is applied to the language. The application of the defined system of gender signs has a number of effects. First, there is a system of verb tenses and transitive-intransitive verb forms that happens in relation to the gender of each letter. Then, the pronunciation of each letter is defined in relation to its gender. Then, the gender of the suffix letters affects their connection to subsequent words. And so on. Like *The Thirty*, the presentation

---

[6] Tib. རྟགས་ཀྱི་འཇུག་པ་, rtags kyi 'jug pa.

[7] Tib. རྟགས་, rtags.

of the body of the text is made via the three main types of letters—prefixes, name-bases, and suffixes—and, also like *The Thirty*, the emphasis is on the fact that the suffixes are key to understanding the language.

5. The Commentaries used Today to Explain Thumi's Treatises

Ever since the ninth century, the treatises of Thumi have formed the basis of explanations of Tibetan grammar. Learned Tibetans have written texts that explained grammar according to their understanding of Thumi's work by explaining their understanding of the meaning of the two existing treatises. However, there were places in Thumi's two treatises where the meaning could be interpreted in varying ways and, on top of that, six of his treatises that contained the definitions of Tibetan grammar were missing, so differences of opinion arose in Tibet over the meaning of various matters of grammar. Thus, there came to be masters who espoused differing views of grammar. They in turn had followers who maintained the views of that master with the result that a number of lineages of Tibetan grammar arose in Tibet during the many centuries following Thumi Saṃbhoṭa's original definition of the grammar.[8]

As the centuries went by in Tibet, there were periods of rise and fall of scholarship. With that, a number of individuals who became important as Tibetan grammarians appeared at the times

---

[8] For a complete listing of the various grammarians who arose in Tibet and explanation of their grammar lineages, see volume one of the standard references to Tibetan grammar mentioned earlier in the introduction.

when scholarship was full of vitality. Of them, the ones whose works and opinions are most popular in our current time appeared in a period of renaissance which began in the 1700's.

The eighth Situ Rinpoche, Situ Chokyi Jungney, was born in Eastern Tibet in the late 1700's. He was a remarkable scholar and a very highly accomplished master of the Karma Kagyu tradition of Tibetan Buddhism. He was a central figure in the renaissance of learning that happened in Tibet during his time, writing prolifically on many subjects in both the inner and outer topics of knowledge. His works on grammar set a new standard in the understanding of grammar and his standard is the one in common use today. His writings and teachings on grammar have earned him the position of one, if not the greatest, of Tibetan grammarians.

In order to master grammar, Situ Rinpoche descended from Tibet to Nepal to learn Sanskrit properly. This might sound like the obvious thing to do for someone wanting to be an expert on Indian grammar, but it is unusual because few Tibetans actually did such a thing, it being a life-threatening proposition (for example, read Marpa Lotsawa's biography, *The Life of Marpa*). After mastering Sanskrit, Situ Rinpoche returned to Tibet and eventually wrote a large commentary on Tibetan grammar named *A Beautiful String of Pearls to Adorn the Necks of the Wise, A Thorough Explanation of the Specific Texts "The Thirty" and "Application of Gender Signs" of the Śhāstras that Authentically Set Forth the Signs of the Snowy Land.* This commentary is the centrepiece of his writings on grammar and is usually referred to as *A Beautiful String of Pearls* or more commonly as *Situ's Great Commentary*[9].

Situ's Great Commentary is an extremely difficult text to follow. There are two reasons for that. Firstly, Situ Rinpoche had a good command of Sanskrit and wrote directly about both Sanskrit and Tibetan grammars throughout his commentary. To understand the commentary, one has to understand both Sanskrit and Tibetan grammar and understand them well. Secondly, his text not only incorporates his view regarding what is correct Tibetan grammar but also puts forth all the necessary arguments to defeat whatever contrary views other grammarians might have put forth. In doing so, he quotes widely from the works of various Tibetan grammarians preceding him so, to follow the text, one has to have a considerable knowledge of the various Tibetan grammatical traditions.

The arguments about grammar amongst Tibetan scholars are mostly founded in differences of opinion that grew up because of the loss of most of Thumi's original treatises, the terseness of Thumi's extant treatises, and the lack of supporting materials from his time. An example of a major point of contention is the debate over how the vowels are defined. Thumi's definition of vowels and consonants refers to the Sanskrit system of vowels and consonants but defines them very differently and only very briefly. Most Western students of Tibetan language these days trot out with complete confidence the formulation that the Tibetan language has five vowels. Amazingly, they do so without even knowing that most Tibetans say there are four because Thumi mentions in his terse definition that there are only four marks for

[9] Tib. སི་ཏུའི་འགྲེལ་ཆེན་, si tu'i 'grel chen.

writing the vowels. Some Western students say that "Tibetan has five vowels, one of them hidden" without realizing that this is a mistaken rehash of Situ Rinpoche's final assessment of the matter and without knowing that many other grammarians disagreed with what Situ did say about it. Situ made many very cogent arguments regarding this and many other matters in his *Great Commentary*. The force of his arguments were so convincing that his system still prevails.

In short, Situ's *Great Commentary* served to give Tibetan grammar a footing that it had lost. The commentary quickly became a key piece of Tibetan literature that caused a revolution of understanding. A new lineage of Tibetan grammar developed from the explanations contained in it.

After Situ had completed his work, there were a few people who argued against it but, having read their works, it seems to me that they were just complaining for political reasons and not because of any substantial argument that they could level against Situ's words. Situ's presentation quickly became the one that was generally followed in Tibet and has stayed that way until the present because of the excellence of the explanations contained in it.[10]

---

[10] Because Situ Rinpoche's *Great Commentary* is considered by many Tibetans to be the ultimate commentary on Tibetan grammar, many Westerners have been wanting to see a translation of it. However, such a thing is very difficult to do. There are very few Tibetans who understand it properly, let alone Westerners. Allow me to say at this point that the current Situ Rinpoche personally asked me to translate this work, offering me all assistance needed and stating that he was very confident that I did have the knowledge needed to do so. His

(continued ...)

During the time of Situ, a very great Gelugpa teacher called Ngulchu Dharmabhadra [1772–1851] made a point of writing several grammar texts. Like Situ Chokyi Jungney, he was deeply concerned at the lack of understanding of grammar that prevailed in his time. He found Situ's explanations to be excellent, so he

---

[10] (... continued)
confidence was based in part on the fact that I have received months of teaching of the entire text, all in Tibetan and in a Tibetan environment, from my own grammar teacher, Padma Gyaltsen, who was regarded at that time as the greatest living Tibetan grammarian. My assessment, with the knowledge that I do have, is that it would not be very useful to do so. Here are two reasons for that assessment.

Firstly, there is the hard fact that much of the content only makes sense in Tibetan; it simply cannot be translated as such into English. It can be explained in English but the explanation could not be a mere re-phrasing of the Tibetan text. What is needed is not a translation of the text but an explanation of it. Accordingly, I have produced major works on Tibetan grammar which do just that. They explain, step by step, all of the details involved with Tibetan grammar, and in doing so, effectively present what is contained in Situ Chokyi Jungney's exceptional work.

Secondly, there is the hard fact that much of the content of *Situ's Great Commentary* is very detailed argument which might be interesting to grammar scholars but will not be of interest to someone who wants to know Tibetan grammar as a practical matter. Moreover, much of this detailed argument can only be understood with a deep understanding of both Sanskrit and Tibetan grammars. Even if someone were interested, he would not be able to understand it simply through a translation of the text. Again a major explanation of Tibetan grammar is required and that is again, exactly what I have produced in my major works on grammar.

wrote a number of texts that presented Situ's understanding and thereby became the first major successor to Situ's views of grammar. In particular, he wrote a text that presented *Situ's Great Commentary* but with all difficult and non-essential material removed. His text, known as *Situ's Words*, presents Situ's understanding of grammar but in a very readable, useful way. He did his work so well that *Situ's Words* became and still is the most widely read text of Tibetan grammar.

Ngulchu Dharmabhadra passed his lineage to his nephew Yangchen Drubpay Dorje [1809–1884] who also wrote several texts on grammar. His texts were very clear and all of them became and still are very popular. Ngulchu Dharmabhadra's writings on grammar were all at the medium to advanced level, so he asked his nephew to write a beginner's-level grammar text that would present their understanding of grammar but be very easy to understand and learn. Yangchen Drubpay Dorje followed this instruction and produced a pair of texts that quickly became the most basic texts for learning grammar. The texts are used by all Tibetans these days as the basic texts for learning grammar.

Other, well-known presentations of grammar have been made since Thumi's time. For example, Sakya Pandita [1182–1251] and Sonam Tsemo [1142–1182] both of the Sakya tradition wrote texts on grammar and followers of the Sakya tradition will sometimes use these for their studies. Similarly, there have been a number of Gelugpa scholars who have written well-known works on grammar[11]. Nonetheless, it is Situ's presentation of

---

[11] A very extensive presentation of the history of grammar in Tibet and the various major grammarians involved can be found in volume (continued ...)

grammar and the presentations of those who followed his way of thought, especially Ngulchu Dharmabhadra and Yangchen Drubpay Dorje, that have become the main texts used for the study of grammar in Tibetan culture. Therefore, I have emphasized their works in my writings on and translations of Tibetan grammar, thinking that their works will be of the greatest benefit to non-Tibetans who are trying to learn Tibetan grammar.

A. Beginner's Level: The *Great Living Tree* Tibetan Grammars

Thumi's defining treatises are not easy to comprehend so are not used as the text-books for the study of the language. Tibetan children begin their education by learning to write the letters and pronounce the sounds of the Tibetan vowels and consonants. They then learn to write words. To go with this, they will usually learn, by heart, an abbreviated text by Yangchen Drubpay Dorje called *"The Great Living Tree", The Essence of Thonmi's Fine Explanation "The Thirty"*, a text which presents the essential meaning of *The Thirty* in a manner suitable for easy memorization.

Like so many other Tibetan texts, it is well-known by its poetic sub-title *The Great Living Tree*, which taken most literally means "the living tree that stands over all others". The author's intent with the words *living tree* is that his text presents the living tradition of grammar and not merely the dead assertions of people who do not really understand the subject. Then, it is the *great*

---

[11] (... continued)
one of the standard references to Tibetan grammar mentioned earlier.

tree amongst the trees in the forest of explanation; it is the one replete with leaves of the finest explanations possible and the fruit of the most enjoyable explanations possible.

To get a full feeling for the title, you have first to understand that he was writing shortly after Situ Chokyi Jungney had done his great work of reviving grammar following a long period of scholastic darkness in Tibet. Yangchen Drubpay Dorje had Situ's lineage of explanation, a lineage that was alive and vital, and which had excellent ways of explanation; it had gone beyond the deadness of understanding coupled with poor explanations which had covered Tibet. Then it has to be understood that Yangchen Drubpay Dorje was a master poet who chose this theme as the one for use throughout his texts on grammar. All in all, the title and theme of the greatest of living trees that explain grammar is a very clever way of expressing the actual situation of his time, and not merely some nice-sounding words for the name of his text.

In short, his *The Great Living Tree* text is like the greatest of living trees in a forest, the one that stands above all others, producing a luxuriant foliage and fruit of excellent explanations of grammar.

The Great Living Tree is a beginner's text. Therefore, it presents a very clear summation of Thumi's first treatise, *The Thirty*, but does not mention the other treatise, *Application of Gender Signs*. This is appropriate. Thumi's first treatise is the basis of Tibetan grammar and needs to be studied in order to know the basics.

The Great Living Tree does have something in it that most other Tibetan grammar texts do not. Neither *The Thirty* nor almost any other Tibetan text contains a guide to the use of punctuation, so *The Great Living Tree* includes some information about the use of the two main punctuation marks, tsheg's and shad's. This again is in keeping with its being a text that provides a beginner with the basics of the language.

The Great Living Tree is a very concise text meant mainly for memorization purposes. It needs explanation to make its meaning clear. Therefore, Yangchen Drubpay Dorje wrote his own commentary to clarify it and called it *"The Fine Explanation Great Living Tree" The Clarifier of the Meaning of The Essence of "The Thirty"*. This commentary, which is well-known by its short title *The Fine Explanation Great Living Tree*[12], takes the root text phrase by phrase and amplifies it to make the meaning clearer.

This pair of texts has been used ever since they were written and still are used to teach the Tibetan language system to beginning students both inside and outside Tibet. As Yangchen Drubpay Dorje says in the colophon to *The Fine Explanation Great Living Tree*:

> This *Clarifier of the Meaning of the Essence of The Thirty* was written to be an easy, condensed explanation of the root, with examples, for those new, young students whose minds could not accommodate a subtle and vast … explanation.

There is a point of grammar in understanding and translating the title correctly. The wording of the title, which can be clearly understood with a good understanding of Tibetan grammar and styles of writing, does not say "Fine Explanation of the Great Living Tree". Rather, it is worded to mean that this is not the

---

[12] Tib. ལེགས་བཤད་ལྗོན་པའི་དབང་པོ་, legs bshad ljon pa'i dbang po.

great living tree itself but another one like it, a fine explanation type of great living tree. With its fine explanation, it makes clear the meaning of the other great living tree, the one which is the essence of *The Thirty*. Thus, the correct understanding of the title is "Fine Explanation Great Living Tree".

There is also a point of learning in understanding the "Great Living Tree" part of both titles. The word « ལྗོན་པ་, ljon pa » in Tibetan means a living tree as opposed to a dead one. This detail has not been well understood amongst non-Tibetans. For example, there is a living tree in the desire god realm, Heaven of the Thirty Three, and one in Amitabha's pure land, Sukhāvati. Some less knowledgeable Western translators have seen the names of these trees and assumed that the word « ལྗོན་པ་, ljon pa » used to indicate those trees must mean a heavenly tree or wish-fulfilling tree of some kind. In fact, « ལྗོན་པ་, ljon pa » simply means a living tree and it is used in the names of those two trees mentioned because the trees are alive and flourishing, no more and no less. Amazingly, this mistaken understanding has now found its way into several dictionaries! And worse, has gone from the dictionaries into further mistaken translations.

B. Medium to Advanced Level: *Situ's Words* and *Essence of the Elegant Explanation*

The most popular text for understanding grammar amongst Tibetans in general and especially amongst those following Situ's system is *The Supremely Learned Situ's Words, A Thorough Explanation of the Grammar Śhāstras of the Language of the Snowy Land, "The Thirty" and "Application of Gender Signs"* by Ngulchu

Dharmabhadra. This title is usually abbreviated to *Situ's Words*[13]. The title means that the text presents the authoritative statements spoken[14] by Situ Rinpoche regarding the two existent treatises of Thumi. *Situ's Words* is an abridgement of *Situ's Great Commentary* that leaves out all the difficult material. Ngulchu Dharmabhadra's excellent understanding of grammar allowed him to abridge the *Great Commentary* in a way that no-one else could. The work is so well done that it has become the standard text for those who want to understand grammar at the level of serious study but who cannot approach the *Great Commentary* because of its complexity and difficulty.

Then there is a grammar text that follows Situ's system but has been in use instead of *Situ's Words* as the standard text for grammar at the seat of the Karma Kagyu lineage, Tsurphu, in Tibet and now Rumtek in Sikkim. The text was written by the Kagyu khenpo called Ngedon Jamyang[15] who lived at Tshurpu in the 19th century. The full title of his commentary is *The Essence of the Elegant "Thorough Explanation", The Literal Aspect of the Snowy Land's Grammar Śhāstras, "The Thirty" and "Application of Gender Signs"*. The words in the title "*Thorough Explanation*" are an abbreviation of the full name of *Situ's Great Commentary*. The title tells exactly what the text is: a condensation of Situ's very elegantly written *Great Commentary* into an essential version of his text that gives the meaning of Thumi's treatises at the literal

---

[13] Tib. སི་ཏུའི་ཞལ་ལུང་, si tu'i zhal lung.

[14] Tib. ཞལ་ལུང་, zhal lung.

[15] Tib. ངེས་དོན་འཇམ་དབྱངས་, nges don 'jam dbyangs.

level[16]. The title is always abbreviated in this book to *Essence of the Elegant Explanation*.

Essence of the Elegant Explanation, like Ngulchu Dharmabhadra's *Situ's Words*, is meant to be an easier-to-understand version of *Situ's Great Commentary*. As with *Situ's Words*, it is in essence a copy of Situ's text with all of the difficult material expunged and with the author's own comments added here and there. As Khenpo Ngedon says in his preface,

> … overall I make a commentary so that beginners can have easy access—since it touches on few difficult matters it is easy to understand. Principally though, it is the words and meanings of *A Thorough Explanation, A Beautiful Pearl Necklace* nicely condensed to their essence and arranged together with examples.

Essence of the Elegant Explanation is very similar to *Situ's Words*, nonetheless Khenpo Ngedon has his own opinion on some things and says things a little differently here and there. As well as that, the khenpo includes detail from *Situ's Great Commentary* that Ngulchu Dharmabhadra leaves out of *Situ's Words*. This makes the khenpo's commentary a useful companion to *Situ's Words*, especially for scholars.

---

[16] "Literal meaning" simply refers to the fact that this is a text written on the straightforward level of meaning and explanation. The Buddhist literary tradition distinguishes various types of explanation of a subject, such as ones that show the literal meaning, the hidden meaning, the ultimate meaning and so on, so here the author is stating which kind of explanation it is.

Texts like *Situ's Words* and *Essence of the Elegant Explanation* are the way to get into serious studies of Tibetan grammar. They provide a very realistic picture of *Situ's Great Commentary* which can be translated in a meaningful way that can be understood by non-Tibetans. I would like to suggest quite strongly to those who want to teach classes in grammar, for instance at the university level in the West or in other study institutions, that *Situ's Great Commentary* is not really very suited to the purpose but that these texts are ideal. This advice echoes the words of my own grammar teacher, Padma Gyaltsen, who said that it would be nice, he supposed, if the *Great Commentary* could be translated, but that it made much more sense to make a good, accessible translation of *Situ's Words*. He felt that *Situ's Words* was the text par excellence for studies of grammar that all but the most determined scholar would want to undertake.

c. Advanced Level Dealing Exclusively with the *Application of Gender Signs*: *A Mirror which Reveals the Difficult Points* and its Commentary

Thumi's *Application of Gender Signs* treatise is considered to be very difficult to understand and certainly not for beginners. Therefore, the beginner's level texts by Yangchen Drubpay Dorje do not deal at all with the topics contained in it. The medium to advanced texts by Ngulchu Dharmabhadra and Khenpo Ngedon Jamyang do explain the treatise and their explanations are good. However, some people want a commentary that deals exclusively with that treatise.

Such commentaries are few in number compared to the mainstream commentaries on grammar that treat both of Thumi's treatises within the one text. To find the ones which are popular today, we turn again to the uncle-nephew lineage of Zhey where we find that Ngulchu Dharmabhadra wrote commentaries that exclusively dealt with the *Application of Gender Signs* and that his nephew and student Yangchen Drubpay Dorje wrote his own texts based on them which, as with his other texts already mentioned, became very popular and have stayed that way. In particular, there is a pair of commentaries from Yangchen Drubpay Dorje that deal solely with *Application of Gender Signs*. Similar to his pair of *Great Living Tree* commentaries, the first commentary is a summary which could easily be committed to memory and the second is a long explanation of that summary. The summary text is called *A Mirror which Reveals the Difficult Points", A Short Statement of the Essential Meaning of "The Application of Gender Signs"* by Yangchen Drubpay Dorje. The commentary to that is called *A Golden Key of Knowledge, Commentary to "A Mirror that Reveals the Difficult Points of 'The Application of Gender Signs'"*. These two texts are considered to be excellent presentations of Thumi's treatise.

6. About the Grammars Presented in this Book

1. The Author

Ngulchu in Central Tibet is famous for its Dharma Fortress[17] hermitage in Zhey[18] which was originally sanctified by the teaching and meditations of Gyalsey Thogmey Palzangpo[19], the eminent Sakya-Kadampa master who lived from 1295 to 1369

[17] Tib. དངུལ་ཆུ་ཆོས་རྫོང་, dngul chu chos rdzong.

[18] Tib. བཞད་, bzhad.

[19] Tib. རྒྱལ་སྲས་ཐོགས་མེད་དཔལ་བཟང་པོ་, rgyal sras thogs med dpal bzangpo.

C.E. and who wrote the very famous and much-used text *The Thirty Seven Practices of Buddha Sons.*

A line of very famous teachers began at the hermitage in the 18th century. The line was called Ngulchu Uncles and Nephews[20] because it consisted of gurus who were uncles and lineage-holding disciples who were nephews from the area. The lineage followed the teachings of the Gelugpa tradition. The first in the line was Jetsun Ngawang Dorje[21] [1720–1803] who was very famous for his meditative attainment. His nephew, disciple, and successor was Dharmabhadra Palzangpo [1772–1851] though he is commonly known as Ngulchu Dharmabhadra[22]. He was one of the most revered Gelugpa lamas of Central Tibet during the first half of the nineteenth century. His nephew, disciple, and successor was Yangchen Drubpay Dorje[23] [1809–1887] who was also known as very learned.

According to tradition, Ngulchu Dharmabhadra was a master scholar of very high meditative attainment and, like the eighth Situ Rinpoche who authored *Situ's Great Commentary*, was a prolific writer who wrote on a wide variety of topics. His extensive writings include several works on grammar and related subjects, all of which are preserved in his *Collected Works* [24]. He

---

[20] Tib. དངུལ་ཆུ་ཁུ་དབོན་, dngul chu khud bon.

[21] Tib. རྗེ་བཙུན་ངག་དབང་རྡོ་རྗེ་, rje btsun ngag dbang rdo rje.

[22] Tib. དྷརྨ་བྷདྲ་དཔལ་བཟང་པོ་, dharma bhadra dpal bzangpo and དངུལ་ཆུ་དྷརྨ་བྷདྲ་, dngul chu dharma bhadra.

[23] Tib. དབྱངས་ཅན་གྲུབ་པའི་རྡོ་རྗེ་, dbyangs can grub pa'i rdo rje.

[24] Tib. གསུང་འབུམ་, gsung 'bum.

is most famous for his text called *Situ's Words* [25] which, as mentioned earlier, presents *Situ's Great Commentary* clearly but with most of the difficult material removed. This and all of his other texts on grammar were written in exact accordance with Situ's position and he became known as the first lineage holder after Situ Rinpoche of Situ's system of grammar. Yangchen Drubpay Dorje followed Ngulchu Dharmabhadra's system exactly and, at his guru's insistence, wrote many books on grammar and other subjects, too. Yangchen Drubpay Dorje's grammars are probably the most widely read Tibetan grammars amongst Tibetans at this time.

ii. How the Grammars Are Presented

The translations of the grammars follow this introduction. Footnotes have not been added to the root text because the commentary to it goes through it, explaining it word by word. However, many footnotes have been added to the commentary text in order to clarify difficult points of both texts.

A glossary has been provided following the commentaries in order to clarify the grammar terms found in the commentaries. It is usual to make a footnote in the texts at the first instance of each term that has been explained in the glossary, but we found that doing so cluttered the already complicated texts so abandoned it. Simply consult the glossary whenever you meet a technical term whose meaning needs clarification. The explanations in the glossary are brief though clear; more extensive explanations of all terms can be found in the standard references to Tibetan grammar mentioned earlier.

---

[25] Tib. སི་ཏུའི་ཞལ་ལུང་, situ'i zhal lung.

Finally, the Tibetan texts are presented to facilitate study.

Note that Tibetan grammar texts are not intended to be do-it-yourself books on grammar. Rather, as with most Tibetan texts, they are meant to provide a written framework for oral instruction, with the oral instruction being the real teaching on the subject.

7. Sanskrit

Sanskrit is represented in this book using the IAST system of transliteration, the system used in most academic circles. This system has been in use for many years and it is nowadays increasingly felt that it could be improved a little. In this book, the following modifications have been made to improve ease of reading and pronunciation:

ṛ is written ṛi
ḷ is written ḷi
ś is written śh
ṣ is written ṣh
ca is written as cha
cha is written as chha

Tony Duff,
Swayambunath,
Nepal,
March 2019

"A MIRROR WHICH REVEALS THE DIFFICULT POINTS" A SHORT STATEMENT OF THE ESSENTIAL MEANING OF *THE APPLICATION OF GENDER SIGNS*

by Yangchen Drubpay Dorje

Namo Mañjuśhrīye

I bow at the feet of the guru who is inseparable from
The delight of the wisdom knowledge of all conquerors
Sporting in the youthful form
Of Jetsun Tenpa'i Khorlo.

The essential meaning of *The Application of Gender Signs*,
The supreme grandmother of grammars that came from
The ocean of the mind of the supreme expert Thonmi,
Will be clarified here in summary form.

Overall, vowels are female and consonants male.
Therefore, the thirty kāli as a whole
Are male letters only and they
Are sub-divided into five sets.

ཀ་, ཅ་, ཏ་, པ, and ཙ་ are male.
ཁ་, ཆ་, ཐ་, ཕ་, and ཚ་ are neutral.

ག་, ཇ་, ད་, བ་, ཛ་, ཝ་, ཞ་,
ཟ་, འ་, ཡ་, ཤ་, and ས་ are female.
ང་, ཉ་, ན་, and མ་ are extremely female.
ར་, ལ་, ཧ་, and ཨ་ are barren and
ཨ་ is also named "characterless".

Of the five prefixes, letter བ་ is male,
ག་ and ད་ are neutral, and འ་ and མ་ are female letters.

For those, which is affixed to which?
Male letter བ་ is affixed to ཀ་, ཅ་, ཏ་,
ཙ་, ག་, ང་, ཇ་, ཉ་, ད་, ན་,
ཛ་, ཞ་, ཟ་, ར་, ཤ་, and ས་.
Neutral ག་ is affixed to ཅ་, ཏ་, ཙ་,
ཉ་, ད་, ན་, ཞ་, ཟ་, ཡ་, ཤ་,
And ས་. Neutral ད་ letter is affixed to
ཀ་, པ་, ག་, བ་, ང་, ན་, and མ་
Female letter འ་ is affixed to ག་, ཇ་, ད་,
བ་, ཛ་, ཁ་, ཆ་, ཐ་, ཕ་, and ཚ་,
And extremely female letter མ་ to
ཁ་, ཆ་, ཐ་, ཚ་, ག་, ཇ་, ད་,
ཛ་, ང་, ཉ་, and ན་.

How do they affix?
Male affixes to a stronger sound effort;
Neutral affixes to a moderate one;
Female in a weaker way; and
Extremely female in flat way.

Why is the affixing done?
To begin with, this has to be understood:
From the standpoint of an agent

In actual relationship to a karma as other,
The two of agent and its instrument
Are the self thing and the two of place of action
And action are the other thing.
No matter how it is—whether there is agent as other like that
Or there is no actual relationship—still, that
The action has been done is the past,
The action will be done is the future, and
The action is being done is the present.
Therefore, the distinction of three tenses
Is present in all spoken constructs
Related to verb function.
The distinction of self-other does not
Pervade merely that, but is a distinction made
In order to include agent and place of action,
One which also includes the action and agent
Related as self and other within it.
Thus it has been stated that the division
Into three tenses not being pervaded by
The distinction into self-other is to be
Understood as the meaning of inclusion.
Still, in the case of the prefix འ་ letter,
Affixation also to the self thing
Connected with mere verb function is seen.

That ascertained, male letter བ་ is affixed
For the past as in བསྒྲུབས་སོ། and
For other thing as in
བསྒྲུབ་བྱའི་ལྷ་, བསྒྲུབ་པར་བྱ་, and so on.

Neutral two ག་ and ད་ are affixed
In གཅོད་པ་པོ་ and གཅོད་པར་བྱེད་,

And གཅོད་པར་འགྱུར་ and དགྲི་བ་པོ་,
And དགྲི་བར་བྱེད་ and དགྲི་བར་འགྱུར་,
And so on to mean self thing and
In གཅད་བྱའི་ཞིང་ and གཅད་པར་བྱ་,
And དགྲི་བྱའི་སྣལ་མ་དགྲི་བར་བྱ་,
And so on to mean other thing and
In གཅོད་བཞིན་པ་ and དགྲི་བཞིན་པ་
And so on, to produce the present.

Female letter འ་ is affixed in འཆད་པ་པོ་,
And འཆད་པར་བྱེད་ and འཆད་པར་འགྱུར་,
And so on for thing of self thing and
In འགྲོ་བ་པོ་ and འགྲོ་བར་བྱེད་
And so on for the meaning of self as complement and
In འཁྲིལ་ལོ་ and so on for the present
And in འཁྲིལ་བར་འགྱུར་ and so on for the future.

The extremely female letter མ་
Is affixed equally for self, other, and the three tenses.
Nonetheless, for the past of an agent in actual
Relationship with other, the འ་ prefix
Certainly not and ག་ and ད་ a little.
For the present, the prefix བ་
A little and for headed present
Not having བ་ fronted is simply certain.
Furthermore, for བ་ fronted forms usually
The agent is included in the present and
The place of action in the future, thus
The past has བ་ fronting and a re-suffix,
The present has neither of the two,
The future has a fronting and no re-suffix, and
The imperative has no fronting and has a re-suffix.

Sometimes past and imperative having
A bare ས་ connected to them also is acceptable.

Of the ten suffix letters,
The four ག་, ད་, བ་ and ས་ are male,
The three ང་, མ་, and འ་ are female,
And the three ན་, ར་, and ལ་ are neutral;
They affix to all name-base letters.

How they affix has two parts:
First, the way of affixation in relation to sound.
The male ག་ letter having a re-suffix
Is the strongest being; male letter བ་
Having a re-suffix is a middling being;
And endings ག་ and བ་ without re-suffix
Or with an ending of ད་ or ས་ are the weakest.
The strong males also are divided into
Three sub-divisions of stronger, weaker, and intermediate.
Similarly, the weak females also are divided into
The two sub-divisions of stronger and weaker;
ང་ and མ་ with re-suffix are female and
ང་ and མ་ without re-suffix or
With འ་ ending are extremely female.
Intermediate neutral ན་, ར་ and ལ་,
Affixed at the end of a name-base male letter
Whether there is a re-suffix or not, and
Affixed after a neutral name-base
When there is a re-suffix,
Are in contact with stronger, so change to stronger.
Affixed after a name-base female letter
When there is no re-suffix,
They are in contact with weaker, so change to weaker.

Those two are changeable neutral.
Affixed after a name-base female letter
When there is a re-suffix,
Because they have both stronger and weaker factors,
They are known as "dual-character neutral".
Affixed after a name-base neutral name-base
When there is no re-suffix,
There is no change at all to stronger or weaker,
So they are asserted to be "characterless neutral".

Second, meaning, has two parts of which
How the prior one will change is concerned with
What the name to which the suffix is joined
Will come to show—self-other, and so on—
Which will usually be known through
The capacity of the prefix joined to that name.
How the subsequent one will be changed is as follows.
Male suffix draws another male at the end of the name,
Female draws a female at the end of the name,
And neutral draws a neutral.
Those ways are the ways of equivalent gender sign being drawn.
There are also very many cases of ease-of-expression being drawn.
Furthermore these items at the end of a name—
The eight cases, the concluders, and so on
With their equivalence of gender or their harmony of sound—
Are drawn according to the force of the prior one.

The particular division of what has been placed—
Either a "case" or "linker"—can be known from the name equivalents resulting from

The connection at the end of that name or phrase.
To explain further, case one expresses
Just the entity of the thing;
Its signifiers, for example like "pot" and "pillar",
Are few in the Tibetan language.
Karma and place of action mean the same;
Showing that some place of an action like that
Has had an action done to it,
Is the second, the objective case and
The second's sub-division, identity.
It is like the fourth, purposiveness's three but for
A place of action that has had an action done to it
Where that or what is connected with it
Is not benefited, that is the second,
For example, like "going to the east".
If there is benefit, it is the fourth,
For example, like "giving to a beggar".
Even if there is no benefit, if the place of action
And the action are of the same entity,
It is the second's sub-division, identity,
For example, like "appeared as the deity".
If there is just the meaning of something which is relying on
Or is positioned on or existing on something else
And otherwise does no specific action,
It is the seventh case, basis,
For example, like "there is a man on top".
If it is like the meaning of the second's time-circumstance,
It is the seventh's sub-division of time-circumstance,
For example, "When the Magha moon appears,
The commemoration of miracles is undertaken".
The terms which elicit cases two, four,
Seven, and time and circumstance, and identity

Are སུ་, ར་, རུ་, དུ་, ན་, ལ་, and ཏུ་,
And given that they usually agree with the ལ་ term
They are also called "the la-equivalent cases".
Nevertheless, it says in the *Speech Door*
That ན་ and ལ་ are not placed for identity.
If the place to which a case is connected
Does an action somewhere far or near,
It is the third one, the agentive case,
For example, "I explained".
If it definitely does no action and
Shows just the making of a connection between former and later,
It is the sixth case, connective term,
For example, like "my eye".
The terms which elicit the third and sixth cases
Are the five གི་, ཀྱི་, གྱི་, འི་, and ཡི་,
With and without a ས་ ending respectively.
If it has the meaning of something that arises from or
Comes out or issues forth from somewhere,
It is the fifth case, source;
For example, "heard from the mouth".
The terms which elicit it are ནས་ and ལས་.
Segregation and inclusion also are included in the fifth.
Furthermore, if the meanings of phrase equivalents
Before and after are to be included,
དང་, ཀྱང་, ཡང་, and འང་, and so on are connected.
If several enumerations repeat the meaning,
The separation-inclusion terms are affixed.
If there are the meanings of negation or
Of owner, then one of the gender signs of the པ་ section
From beginning to end as appropriate is affixed.
Phrase linkers that become ornaments also

Are connected if there is a follow-up to their meaning.
Likewise, if there is more to be shown,
A continuative term is connected.
When a phrase equivalent is complete,
The concluder terms are connected.

Why do they need to be affixed?
If it is not associated with a female letter, a vowel,
Then a male letter, a consonant, cannot be expressed.
Therefore, it is convenient to assert five vowels.
Moreover, for such male letters having a vowel,
If it does not have one of the ten suffixes affixed, then
The meaning carried by the names which show just the entity, and
The distinctions of the names' meaning shown by the phrases, and
The verbal expressions that convey such meanings would not exist.
It is so, because names are drawn out from the letters,
Phrases are drawn out from the names,
And by phrases, the meanings are shown.
If there were no names, phrases, or expressions,
The teaching of ordinary and extraordinary
Knowables also would become non-existent.
Therefore may this, spoken following
The Noble Land's experts,
Be realized by all beings.

It seems like this is just a pile of terminology and words
But an enormous meaning is distinguished within it.
Rely on a correct understanding of language then
Remain in seeking out without mistake what is meaningful!

It is well-known that the experts say that anyone who
Is not expert whether he is ignorant to the meaning or not,
Who follows this approach will be someone who
"Knowing terms has no ignorance".
Anyone who has not learned the subject here and who is
measured as being ignorant of it,
Who enters an institution of exposition, debate, and
composition,
Will, like a fox in lion's clothing,
Sooner or later be revealed.
Therefore, to you who seek a clear intellect,
I say, "Hey! Come quick and look at the image
In this mirror that clearly displays all reflections
Of the difficult points of the *Application of Gender Signs*!"

If errors have accumulated in here,
They are confessed right here in view of the experts.
By the virtue obtained from this small effort,
May all comprehend the meaning of this.

This "Mirror Which Reveals the Difficult Points", A Short Statement of the Essential Meaning of *The Application of Gender Signs*, was composed by myself, Yangchen Drubpay Dorje, according to the needs of my own students Jedrung Sangay Gyatso and Dondrup Phuntshog in accordance with the assertions of the supreme expert Situ Panchen and the All-knowing Dharmabhadra Palzangpo.

"A GOLDEN KEY OF KNOWLEDGE" COMMENTARY TO "A MIRROR WHICH REVEALS THE DIFFICULT POINTS OF *THE APPLICATION OF GENDER SIGNS*"

by Yangchen Drubpay Dorje

Namo Mañjuśhrīye
Homage to Mañjuśhrī

The dharma that is the innate disposition of the pervasive
knowables in their entirety
Seen directly in the inexpressible, unchanging dhātu,
Is the guardian who kindness is even more than that of all the
conquerors,
The conqueror at the crown of the kings of dharma who teach
the Buddha Word.[26]

This, all the wisdoms without exception of the conquerors of
the three times

[26] The verse here is the standard verse prelude that gives a context to the text. It is called the expression of worship and usually contains a homage to those who, preceding the author, have conveyed the knowledge to be discussed in the text. This first verse speaks of the ultimate wisdom of all the buddhas, the dharmakāya which is the source of all knowledge in the world, including the knowledge of grammar.

Condensed into one, is its self-expression in form, the deity of speech,
Who plays with the beguiling dance of two eights' youth:
Mañjuśhrī Vajratikṣhṇa, please bestow goodness and virtue".[27]

The melody of all maṇḍalas which comes forth like
A tamboura giving the eighty-four thousand dharmas,
The beautiful lady so delightful for the fortunate to hear,
Devi of sounds, Oh, play in my heart![28]

The vajra of profound and vast intellect come about in Sarasvati's mind
Is the pleasure garden of the higher levels and within it,
The nicely-made but closed lotus of the *Application of Gender Signs*
Will be opened by the appearance of the sun of fine analysis.[29]

---

[27] The second verse speaks of the saṃbhogakāya manifestation, the form of the dharmakāya. Since the subject here is study in general, the specific sambhogakāya that is mentioned is the speech aspect of the dharmakāya, Mañjuśhrī. Mañjuśhrī in general is said to be at the fullest bloom of youth, and technically speaking that means that he has all sixteen (or two sets of eight) factors of the subtle body fully mature. The saṃbhogakāya here is Mañjuśhrī Vajratikṣhṇa, a form of Mañjuśhrī connected with the incisive knowledge of learning.

[28] When this sharpness of Mañjuśhrī Vajratikṣhṇa's intelligence appears to teach, it often comes as the melodious sound presented by the utterly graceful female form of it, called Sarasvati. The third verse is thus about Sarasvati, the female counterpart of Mañjuśhrī.

[29] The first line of the fourth verse is very cleverly crafted to include both his own and his guru's names as well as Sarasvati's. Thus, his guru and himself both become Sarasvati, who will so elegantly and

(continued ...)

Hey! You six-legged, youthful ones of clear intellect
If you would like to enjoy the feast of honey of the correctly-stated aspects of language,
When the mouth, the doorway, of the flower of elegant explanations opens,
It is right that you should be inside with melodious songs of joy![30]

Now, for the main presentation[31]. There is an amazingly clear presentation of grammar by the great paṇḍita of the degenerate

---

[29] (... continued)
graciously present the intelligence of Mañjuśhrī. The guru's mind, which embodies Sarasvati's mind, here is the pleasure park of the higher realms of saṃsāra filled with flowers trumpeting the elegant explanations of excellent intellect for the sake of the visitors.

[30] The visitors enticed by it are people like ourselves who come in the form of six-legged ones, the bees. We, the young, clear-minded bees, with youth like Mañjuśhrī's, are told that we should come inside the flower whose mouth, the doorway to this elegant explanation of this difficult subject of grammar, is being opened right now and to buzz around, happily enjoying the feast of learning being provided!

One mark of a learned being in India and Tibet is the ability to write poetry. Yangchen Dorje's poetry is really outstanding. He might not have been quite as learned as some others but his way with words, as can be seen in this and his other grammar texts, is truly pleasing, as can be seen from this prelude.

[31] Following the verse prelude, it is customary to shift into prose and introduce the text in that. The words footnoted here are a formula used by nearly all writers that indicates that the transition to the prose is being made.

times, Ngulchu Yangchen Drubpay Dorje Palzangpo[32], called *A Mirror that Reveals the Difficult Points of the "Application of Gender Signs"*. When the extensive divisions into topics of that text are left out and it is explained in a summarized form, there are just three main headings:

I. The Expression of Worship
II. The Declaration of Composition
III. The Actual Text

I. The Expression of worship

The expression of worship is done via both Indian and Tibetan languages so has two parts.

a. ***Via Indian language:***

The text says:

Namo Mañjuśhrīye

There is the northern Snowy Land with its various parts[33]: the reservoir-like Tripartite Ngari Region to the east; the aqueduct-like four-sectioned Central Tibet and Tsang in the centre; and

---

[32] This is the name of his guru, who was famous for his text on grammar called *Situ's Words* as well as other texts on grammar and language including one on the difficult points of the *Application of Gender Signs*, the name of which he mentions here. This text on the same subject by Yangchen Drubpay Dorje follows his guru's text, but is a simplified form designed to be easier to understand.

[33] Meaning greater Tibet. Greater Tibet has three main parts: western, central, and eastern which are mentioned here in that order.

the field-like six-highlands of Do Kham to the West. This place is also divided into Tibet and Greater Tibet and of the language of those two, here in the language of Tibet—which is the language of Central Tibet and Tsang—"namo" is "I prostrate", "mañju" is "gentled", "śhrī" is "glory", and "ye" is "to", so it is "I prostrate to Mañjuśhrī[34]".

b. ***Via Tibetan language:***

The text says:

> I bow at the feet of the guru who is inseparable from
> The delight of the wisdom knowledge of all
> conquerors
> Sporting in the youthful form
> Of Jetsun Tenpa'i Khorlo.

This is saying, "The essence of that delight which is the condensation into one place of the total knowledge of the wisdom of all the conquerors of the universes, sporting in the youthful, sixteen-year old form, is Jetsun Tenpa'i Khorlo[35], that is, Mañjuśhrīghoṣha. I bow with very reverent three doors at the lotus feet of the actual and lineage gurus, Dharmabhadra[36] and so on, the omniscient ones who un-mistakenly show paths to the higher rebirths and

---

[34] Mañjuśhrī's name, literally Gentled Glory in English, is explained to mean that his mind *has been made gentle* by removal of all the obscurations and the afflictions they entail and he has the *glory* of fully enacting the two aims of himself and others.

[35] "Tenpa'i Khorlo" ia another name for Mañjuśhrī Vajratikṣhṇa, who is one of the many aspects of Mañjuśhrīghoṣha, the general name for the sambhogakāya form of the speech of the buddhas.

[36] This is another common name for his guru, Ngulchu Yangchen Drubpay Dorje Palzangpo.

definite goodness[37] and who are inseparable with Jetsun Tenpa'i Khorlo."

II. The Declaration of Composition

The text says:

> The essential meaning of *The Application of Gender Signs*,
> A supreme grandmother of grammars that came from
> The ocean of the mind of the supreme expert Thonmi,
> Will be clarified here in summary form.

This is saying, "Constellations of learned and accomplished ones have come to this snowy region, a place of the medicinal and fragrant Sāla tree[38], and of them, the supreme one is Thonmi[39] himself. Of all the treatises of the grammar of the Snowy Land that came from the great ocean of his mind, the ones that became the grandmothers of all others, the original ones, the bases, or the

---

[37] "Definite goodness" is the fruition of the Buddhist dharma path. It is the goodness of enlightenment which, because there is no falling back from it, is called "definite".

[38] The Sāla tree was famous in the Buddha's time in India. It is a tree that yields herbal substances used for both incense and medicine. The tree also grows in Tibet.

[39] Thonmi is another name for Thumi Saṃbhoṭa. In most earlier writings, he was called "Thumi" meaning the man from the "Thu" clan. Later, he was called "Thonmi", meaning the man from the aread called "Thon". The first volume of the standard references to Tibetan grammar gives an extensive account of him and his names.

roots were *The Thirty* and *Gender Signs*. Of these, the essential meanings of the *Application of Gender Signs* will be made clear in words that are brief but leave nothing out."

III. The Actual Text

1. The explanation of the overall divisions of gender signs of the name-base letters[40]

The text says:

> Overall, vowels are female and consonants male.
> Therefore, the thirty kāli as a whole …

This is saying, "Overall, when letters are categorized, there are two types: vowels and consonants. Of them, the vowels, whose function is signified by the four marks of gigu for the ཨི་ sound, zhabkyu for the ཨུ་ sound, drengbu for the ཨེ་ sound, and naru for the ཨོ་ [41] sound, are understood to be female. And, the distinguishing letters whose function is signified by the thirty marks of the kāli—the thirty letters from ཀ་ to ཨ་— are understood to be male.[42]"

---

[40] The name-base letters are those consonants which can be used as the base letter around which a grammatical name is created. For grammatical name, see the glossary.

[41] The four vowels in Tibetan are the sounds represented roughly in English by i, u, e, and o. The marks that signify them in Tibetan are named gigu, zhabkyu, dengbu, and naro respectively.

[42] What we call "consonants" in English are called "distinguishers" in Tibetan; each one distinguishing a particular sound of the

(continued ...)

The text says:

> Are male letters only and they
> Are sub-divided into five sets.

If the male letters, which are those thirty consonants, are then divided up into the groups that are their sub-divisions, there are five of them. What are the five? They are: male, neutral, female, extremely female, and barren. The term "only" has the meaning "exclusively". Of the five groups, the first ones are the males. The text says:

> ཀ་, ཅ་, ཏ་, པ, and ཙ་ are male.

The five letters ཀ་, ཅ་, ཏ་, པ, and ཙ་ are the male letters. For the second group, the text says:

> ཁ་, ཆ་, ཐ་, ཕ་, and ཚ་ are neutral.

The five letters ཁ་, ཆ་, ཐ་, ཕ་, and ཚ་ are the neutral letters. For the third group, the text says:

> ག་, ཇ་, ད་, བ་, ཛ་, ཝ་, ཞ་,
> ཟ་, འ་, ཡ་, ཤ་, and ས་ are female.

The twelve letters ག་, ཇ་, ད་, བ་, ཛ་, ཝ་, ཞ་, ཟ་, འ་, ཡ་, ཤ་, and ས་ are the female letters. For the fourth group, the text says:

> ང་, ཉ་, ན་, and མ་ are extremely female.

The four letters ང་, ཉ་, ན་, and མ་ together are the extremely female letters. For the fifth group, the text says:

---

[42] (... continued)
language. What we call "vowels" in English are then defined as tones that are vocalized on top of the distinct sounds of the consonants in order to modify and give final form to them.

> ར་, ལ་, ཧ་, and ཨ་ are barren and …

The four letters ར་, ལ་, ཧ་, and ཨ་ together are the barren letters. Then the text says:

> ཨ་ is also named "characterless".[43]

which is saying, "ཨ་ is not only a barren letter but, since it has a sound effort[44] that is extremely weak, it is also named, that is, called, 'characterless'[45]".

---

[43] This is not another category of gender but an alternative name for this member of the barren category. It is given this name in addition to the name "barren" because the vocal effort needed to produce its sound is even weaker than the others in the barren category. It is the weakest of all name-base letters and is so weak that it cannot be typified or characterized so is also called "characterless".

[44] "Sound effort" is an abbreviation of the Tibetan term "sgra gdangs dang byed rtsol ba". The first term "sgra gdangs" means the pronounced sound, how something is vocalized. The second term "byed rtsol ba" means the production effort. The science of pronunciation of the Sanskrit Indian language and of Tibetan following it defines the vocalization of a letter as having three factors: the producer, production place, and production effort. The production effort is an umbrella category for all of the things involved in making the sound other than the actual physical place and the producers (for example, the palate is one place and the tongue is one producer). In this case, it is referring specifically to the strength of these efforts, that is, how forcefully the vocalization is done. The term is used throughout this text and all other texts discussing these matters.

[45] This is not another category of gender but an alternative name for this member of the barren category. It is given this name in addition to the name "barren" because its sound effort is even weaker again

(continued ...)

2. The explanation of the divisions of the gender signs of the prefixes

The text says:

> Of the five prefixes, letter བ་ is male …

Five letters are pre-affixed to their recipient name-bases. As it says in *The Fine Explanation Great Living Tree* grammar text, "ག་, ད་, བ་, མ་, and འ་ are prefixes", thus the text says:

> ག་ and ད་ are neutral, and འ་ and མ་ are female letters.

Both ག་ and ད་ are neutral prefixes. When it says, "འ་ and མ་ are female letters" it means that both are female but འ་ is simply female and མ་ is extremely female.

3. The explanation of the affixation of the gender signs of the prefixes

The text says:

> For those, which is affixed to which?

This is saying, "For those letters explained immediately above, which prefix is affixed to which name-base letter?" The text says:

> Male letter བ་ is affixed to ཀ་, ཅ་, ཏ་,
> ཙ་, ག་, ང་, ཇ་, ཉ་, ད་, ན་,

[45] (... continued)
than the others in the barren category; it is the weakest of all name-base letters and is so weak that it cannot be typified, hence is also called "characterless".

ཛ་, ཞ་, ཟ་, ར་, ཤ་, and ས་.

The prefix male letter བ་ is affixed to these sixteen letters: ཀ་, ཅ་, ཏ་, ཙ་, ག་, ང་, ཇ་, ཉ་, ད་, ན་, ཛ་, ཞ་, ཟ་, ར་, ཤ་, and ས་. And, it is affixed to them as follows. To:

ཀ་ in the three cases of being bare, super-fixed, and sub-fixed e.g., བཀའ། བསྐ། བཀྱེ། བཀྲ། བསྐྱངས།;

ཅ་ only as a fronting[46] to the bare letter e.g., བཅས། བཅོམ། བཅུག;

ཏ་ in the two cases of being bare and super-fixed e.g., བཏབ། བཏུད། བཏགས། བརྟགས། བལྟ། བསྟར།;

ཙ་ bare and super-fixed as in བཙལ། བཙོས། བརྩུགས། བརྩེགས།;

ག་ in the three cases of being bare, super-fixed, and sub-fixed as in བགོ། བགྲང་། བགྱིས། བརྒྱལ། བསྒོམས།;

ང་ only as a fronting to the super-fixed letter as in བརྔམས། བསྔགས།;

ཇ་ only as a fronting to the super-fixed letter as in བརྗེས། བརྗིད།;

ཉ་ only as a fronting to the super-fixed letter as in བརྙན། བསྙེན།;

ད་ in the two cases of being bare and super-fixed as in བདེ། བརྡ། བལྡག བསྡད།;

ན་ only as a fronting to the super-fixed letter as in བརྣག བསྣམས།;

ཛ་ only as a fronting to the super-fixed letter as in བརྫེས། བརྫིས།;

ཞ་ only as a fronting to the bare letter as in བཞག བཞི། བཞེས།;

---

[46] For the terms fronting, super-fix, sub-fix, and bare letter, see the glossary.

ཟ་ in two cases of bare and sub-fixed e.g., བཟང་། བཟི། བཟུང་། བཟེད། བཟོ། བཟླས།;

ར་ only as a fronting to the sub-fixed letter as in བརླབས།;

ཤ་ only as a prefix to the bare letter as in བཤད། བཤེས།;

ས་ in the two cases of being bare and sub-fixed as in བསམ། བསུ། བསེ། བསོས། བསྲིས། བསྲུངས། བསྲེས། བསྲོས།.

Then the text says:

> Neutral ག་ is affixed to ཅ་, ཏ་, ཙ་,
> ཉ་, ད་, ན་, ཞ་, ཟ་, ཡ་, ཤ་,
> And ས་ …

The prefix neutral ག་ is affixed to the eleven name-bases ཅ་, ཏ་, ཙ་, ཉ་, ད་, ན་, ཞ་, ཟ་, ཡ་, ཤ་, and ས་ only as a fronting to the bare letter as in གཅོད། གཏེར། གཙོ། གཉེན། གདོང་། གནད། གཞལ། གཟིགས། གཡང་། གཤེགས། གསུང་།.

Then the text says:

> Neutral ད་ letter is affixed to
> ཀ་, པ་, ག་, བ་, ང་, ན་, and མ་.

The prefix neutral ད་ letter is affixed to the six name-bases ཀ་, པ་, ག་, བ་, ང་, ན་, and མ་. Moreover, it is affixed to ང་ only as a fronting to the bare letter and to the other five both bare and sub-fixed as in དཀར། དཀྱིལ། དཀྲིགས། དཔལ། དཔྲལ། དཔྱིད། དགའ། དགྲ། དགྱེས། དབང་། དབྲི། དབྱིབས། དངུལ། དམའ། དམིགས། དམྱལ།.

Then the text says:

> Female letter འ་ is affixed to ག་, ཇ་, ད་,
> བ་, ཛ་, ཁ་, ཆ་, ཐ་, ཕ་, and ཚ་ …

The female འ་ letter is affixed to the ten letters ག་, ཇ་, ད་, བ་, ཛ་, ཁ་, ཆ་, ཐ་, ཕ་, and ཚ་ of which it is affixed to:

ག་ both bare and sub-fixed འགའ། འགྲོ། འགྲེལ།;
ཇ་ fronted to the bare letter འཇལ།;
ད་ both bare and sub-fixed འདབ། འདྲི། འདྲ།;
བ་ bare and sub-fixed e.g., འབའ། འབྲོག འབྱོར།;
ཛ་ fronted to the bare letter འཛེར། འཛུམ། འཛོལ།;
ཁ་ bare and sub-fixed འཁོར། འཁྲུལ། འཁྲི། འཁྲིར།;
ཆ་ fronted to the bare letter འཆད། འཆང་། འཆར།;
ཐ་ fronted to the bare letter འཐོབ།;
ཕ་ bare and sub-fixed འཕར། འཕྲེང་། འཕྱི།; and
ཚ་ fronted to the bare letter as in འཚོལ།.

Then the text says:

> And extremely female letter མ་ to
> ཁ་, ཆ་, ཐ་, ཚ་, ག་, ཇ་, ད་,
> ཛ་, ང་, ཉ་, and ན་.

The prefix extremely female མ་ letter is affixed to the eleven name-bases ཁ་, ཆ་, ཐ་, ཚ་, ག་, ཇ་, ད་, ཛ་, ང་, ཉ་, and ན་. Of them, it is affixed to both ཁ་ and ག་ bare and sub-joined and to the others fronted to the bare letter e.g., མཁའ། མཁྲིས། མཁྱེན། མཆིས། མཐོང་། མཚུངས། མགོན། མགྲིན། མགྱོགས། མཇལ། མདའ། མཛོད། མངའ། མཉམ། མནན།.

The text says:

> How do they affix?
> Male affixes to a stronger sound effort;
> Neutral affixes to a moderate one;
> Female in a weaker way, and
> Extremely female in flat way.

This is saying, "If you ask, "How are do they become affixed in relation to sound effort?", then the following explanation is given. The prefix male བ་, affixed to its recipient name-base letters[47] has a pronounced, that is, spoken sound, that is greater, and an effort where effort refers to the efforts of breath and so on[48], that is extremely great, hence its affixation creates a stronger sound effort. The affixation of the two neutrals ག་ and ད་ gives a sound effort that is of equal parts, one that is moderate or in-between the other two extremes. The affixation of the female འ་ letter creates a sound effort that is done in a weaker or lesser way. The extremely female མ་ letter has a sound effort that is weaker again than the female, that is, extremely weak, so its affixation results in a flatness of sound."

The text says:

> Why is the affixing done?

What is the necessity behind affixing those five prefixes to their recipient name-base letters, that is, why is it done?

> To begin with, this has to be understood:
> From the standpoint of an agent

---

[47] For recipient letter see the glossary. The term as used here simply means those name-base letters onto which the prefix can be fronted according to the rules of gender.

[48] These are the production efforts referred to earlier. There are many of them, including the degree of breath, that is, aspiration needed to produce the sound, and so on. In this case, it is the strength that is used at the time of pronunciation that is the particular effort being referred to. Degrees of that effort are defined according to the prefix that is fronted to a name-base.

In actual relationship to a karma[49] as other,
The two of agent and its instrument
Are the self thing and the two of place of action
And action are the other thing.

In order to come to a precise understanding of the meaning of Thumi's treatise that is explained under the heading "Why is the affixing of the prefixes done?", it is necessary to first understand this. If there is a karma, that is, an object of an action, that has some action that is to be done to it, then the distinctions of self-other and the three tenses are engaged; whereas if there is no karma, that is, no object of an action that has some action that is to be done to it, then the distinctions of self-other and the three tenses are not engaged.[50]

---

[49] "Karma" is a Sanskrit term generally meaning an action done. In both Sanskrit and Tibetan grammar, it is also used to mean "the site at which a transitive verb action is carried out". In native Tibetan terms, it is the "place of the action". It is not the same as the "object" of the action because in Tibetan verb theory the object of a transitive action has two aspects two it: one is the thing which is the site of the action, and the other is the completion of the action belonging to that site. I have deliberately left it as "karma" because the Tibetans use the Sanskrit word in their own grammar and, as well as that, the same word in Tibetan is used to indicate the verbal action of both transitive and intransitive verbs. This multiple use of terms makes these texts very difficult to read, even for Tibetans!

[50] Self-other is the terminology used in Tibetan grammar to demark the two sides of a transitive verb's action. In English, we refer to subject and object of a transitive action; in Tibetan grammar, one refers to self and other as the two sides of the same. In both languages, a "complement", which is the instrument used to carry out a transitive verbal action, might or might not be present. This

(continued ...)

In regard to that, from the standpoint of the agent being in actual relationship with an other there is the following. Both the agent and the instrument that it uses to do the action are, out of the two possibilities of self and other, self, and if we use a person who cuts wood to illustrate this, then the agent is the person and the instrument used to do the action is the axe. Both the thing which is the place of the action carried out by them and the action that will be carried out by them are, out of the two possibilities of self and other, other. Moreover, the thing which is the place of the action is the wood and the action is the work of cutting the wood: the chopping of the axe; the splitting of the wood into pieces; and so on.

For an example, terms like ཤིང་གཅོད་པ་པོ། ཤིང་གཅོད་པོ། both meaning "the one who cuts wood" produce the understanding of the agent, a person who cuts wood and thereby, out of the two, self and other, it is self. Terms like གཅོད་པར་བྱེད། གཅོད་དོ། "cutting" are called "the term that distinguishes the verb function". The instrument that in fact does that work, the axe, and its action of chopping up and down are to be understood, out of the two self and other, also as self. Various different expressions such as གཅད་བྱ། གཅད་པར་བྱ་བ། གཅད་བྱའི་ཤིང་། "that to be

---

[50] (... continued)
paragraph defines a transitive verbal action as one in which the place of the action has something done to it by another agent—called the "self"—and an intransitive one as one in which there is no other agent doing an action on the place of the action. This clearly settles the argument over whether transitive and intransitive verb definitions are the same in Tibetan and English. At this level, they are. Though further reading will uncover the fact that transitive verb expressions in Tibetan can convey an extra level of meaning that is cannot be conveyed in English.

cut", "what will be cut", and "the wood to be cut" appear but have the same meaning and are called "terms that distinguish the place of the action". In this case, the place of the action is understood to be the wood and out of the two, self and other, is other. Terms like གཅད་པར་བྱ། གཅད་དོ། "will be cut" are called "terms that distinguish the action connected with the place of the action". In this case, it is understood as the axe's action of chopping having actually happened on the wood with the result that wood has split and gone to pieces, etcetera, and out of the two, self and other, is other.

After that kind of distinction between self and other has been grasped conceptually, there is the division into three tenses to be considered. The text says:

> No matter how it is—whether there is agent as other
> like that
> Or there is no actual relationship—still, that
> The action has been done is the past,
> The action will be done is the future, and
> The action is being done is the present.

In regard to the above division into self and other, regardless of how it is in any given circumstance—whether it has an agent in actual relationship to other or not—still, the action will be one of past, present, or future. If the action has been done, it is the past, for example: ལྷ་བསྒྲུབས། "has accomplished the deity", ཤིང་བཅད། "has cut the wood". If the action will be done, it is future, and all of the following are examples of the future tense: ལྷ་བསྒྲུབ། "will accomplish the deity", བསྒྲུབ་པར་བྱ། "will be accomplished", བསྒྲུབ་བྱ། "that to be accomplished", བསྒྲུབ་བྱའི་ལྷ། "deity that will be accomplished", གཅད་བྱ། "that to be cut", གཅད་པར་བྱ་བ། "will be cut", གཅད་པར་བྱ། "will be cut", གཅད་དོ། "will be cut", and གཅད་བྱའི་ཤིང་།

"wood that will be cut". If the action is being done, it is the present, for example: ལྷ་སྒྲུབ། "is accomplishing the deity", སྒྲུབ་བོ། "is accomplishing", སྒྲུབ་བཞིན་པ། "is accomplishing"[51], སྒྲུབ་གྱིན་འདུག "is accomplishing", སྒྲུབ་པར་བྱེད། "is accomplishing", སྒྲུབ་བྱེད། "accomplisher", ཤིང་གཅོད་པར་བྱེད། "is cutting wood", གཅོད་དོ། "cutting", གཅོད་བྱེད། "cutter", གཅོད་བཞིན་པ། "cutting"[52], and གཅོད་གྱིན་འདུག "cutting".

Further, there is the slogan "the three—action, agent, and karma". Each item in it must be identified and the whole understood well, therefore the following is given. Terms like གཅོད་པོ། སྒྲུབ་པ་པོ། "the cutter" and "the accomplisher" are, out of the three—action, agent, and karma—the agent. Terms like གཅོད་པར་བྱེད། གཅད་པར་བྱ། གཅད་དོ། སྒྲུབ་པར་བྱེད། བསྒྲུབ་པར་བྱ། བསྒྲུབ་བོ། "is cutting", "will be cut", "will cut", "is accomplishing", "will be accomplished", "will accomplish", are, out of the three—action, agent, and karma—what is called "the action". Terms like གཅད་བྱ། གཅད་པར་བྱ་བ། གཅད་བྱའི་ཤིང་། བསྒྲུབ་བྱ། བསྒྲུབ་པར་བྱ་བ། བསྒྲུབ་བྱའི་ལྷ། "that to be cut", "what will be cut", "the wood to be cut", "that to be accomplished", "the deity to be accomplished" are, out of the three—action, agent, and karma—what is called "the karma"; this is so because further down in this treatise[53] it says, "karma and place of action mean the same."

---

51 Present continuous tense.

52 Present continuous tense.

53 Meaning the one by his guru which he is currently commenting on.

Furthermore, the doer[54] has two parts, principal and complement: the གཅོད་པ་པོ་ agent who cuts, the person who is a woodcutter, is the principal, and the གཅོད་བྱེད་ cutter, the axe, is the complement. Then, the action is that the wood will be cut and in regard to that there is both the action belonging to the agent and the action belonging to the place of the action. The effort of the axe cutting the wood belongs to the agent, the woodsman, and the term that distinguishes that is གཅོད་པར་བྱེད་ "doing of the cutting". The part that the wood has been cut into pieces belongs to the place of the action, the wood, and the term that distinguishes it is གཅད་དོ། གཅད་པར་བྱ། "the cutting that will happen". There are many different ways of asserting this, with each expert having his own way of doing it, but I think that this one, which is our system, is fitting.

Then, the "thing" mentioned above in "is the self thing", is not explicitly mentioned in the root text *Application of Gender Signs*, so it will be easier for newcomers if this point of understanding is not brought up yet. And with this I must say that talk of "thing which is comprised of both thing and having a thing" is nothing but being overly picky[55].

The text says:

> Therefore, the distinction of three tenses

---

[54] The text has བྱེད་པ་ meaning the thing, overall, that does the action. It effectively means "the agent, the self thing".

[55] This kind of statement is made in relation to the "thing" of Tibetan grammar by people who get into details for the sake of it and who are very narrow in outlook. If one hears this kind of talk, one should leave it alone because it will not help to further a clear understanding of this topic.

> Is present in all spoken constructs
> Related to verb function.

This is saying, "For that reason, the distinction into three tenses is present in every spoken construct that is related to verb function". Or, if we put this in a way that is easy to understand, it is saying, "All spoken constructs related with verb function must either be the past tense or the future tense or the present tense."

The text says:

> The distinction of self-other does not
> Pervade merely that, but is a distinction made
> In order to include agent and place of action,
> One which also includes the action and agent
> Related as self and other within it.

This is saying, "The distinction of self-other does not pervade merely that, the distinction of three tenses being present in every spoken construct connected with verb function."[56] Well then, we could ask, "Where does it not pervade?" In cases like གདུགས་སུ་འཁྱིར། "twirling the umbrella", ཆུར་འཁྱིལ། "swirling into the water" the distinction of three tenses pervades but the distinction of self-other does not; thus it is not incorporated within the distinction of self-other. The point of making the self-other distinction is that it is made for cases like སྒྲུབ་པ་པོ། "accomplisher" and བསྒྲུབ་བྱའི་ལྷ། "deity to be accomplished" where it is made in order to include both the agent and place of the action. And, by the way, the

---

[56] In other words, one of the three tenses is present in every construct that has a verb, but that does not mean that every spoken construct with a verb also has the distinction into self and other in it.

respective, equivalent-force words for the action and agent in self-other relationship are also included within it."

You might think, "How do the equivalent-force terms of the action and agent get included within self-other?" The wording "སྒྲུབ་པར་བྱེད་" is equivalent in force to "སྒྲུབ་པ་པོ་" so, out of the two self and other, it has been included within self. The wording "བསྒྲུབ་པར་བྱ་" is equivalent in force to "བསྒྲུབ་བྱའི་ལྟ་" so, out of the two self and other, it has been included in other.

Then, you might think, "If the distinction of self-other were not made, what would happen?" If it were not made, there would be a problem like this: for example, in སྐལ་ལྡན་གྱིས་སངས་རྒྱས་བསྒྲུབས་ལྟ་བུའི་ཚེ། "At such time as fortunate ones have accomplished buddhahood" the word "བསྒྲུབས་" alone can convey the past tense, but there is the problem that the doubt, "How is it with སྐལ་ལྡན་ 'fortunate ones' and how is it སངས་རྒྱས་ 'buddhahood' will occur?" Making the distinction of self-other results in སྐལ་ལྡན་ "fortunate ones" being the agent in self and སངས་རྒྱས་ "buddhahood" being the action that will have been accomplished in other. That has with it the ease of comprehension needed, and for that reason the distinction self and other is made.

The text says:

> Thus it has been stated that the distinction
> Into three tenses not being pervaded by
> The distinction into self-other is to be
> Understood as the meaning of inclusion.
> Still, in the case of the prefix འ་ letter,
> Affixation also to the self thing
> Connected with mere verb function is seen.

This is saying, "Thus, it has been stated that the need for the division into three tenses of past, future, and present is that it is not pervaded by, that is to say, does not include, the division into self-other which inclusion is to be understood as meaning inclusion in the past tense as in ལྕགས་གསེར་དུ་བསྒྱུར་ "iron become gold", the future tense as in ཆུ་འཁྱིལ་བར་འགྱུར་ "water will swirl", and the present tense as in གདུགས་འཁྱིལ་བྱིན་འདུག "twirling the umbrella", འཁྱིལ་བཞིན་པའོ། "swirling". Still, in the case of the prefix འ་ letter, affixation also with the self thing related with mere verb function, as in ཆོས་འཆད་པ་པོ། "expositer of dharma" and འཆད་པར་བྱེད། "expositer", is seen."

The text says:

> That ascertained, male letter བ་ is affixed …

This is saying, "Now that the correct approach, just explained, has been ascertained, the prefix male letter བ་ is affixed for both past tense and other. To give examples …":

> For the past as in བསྒྲུབས་སོ། and …

For the past as in བསྒྲུབས་སོ། བཀང་། བཅད།. Now that it has been illustrated with those, you should go on to learn it more extensively. Then the text says:

> For other thing as in
> བསྒྲུབ་བྱའི་ལྷ་, བསྒྲུབ་པར་བྱ་, and so on.

The male letter as in བསྒྲུབ་བྱའི་ལྷ་, བསྒྲུབ་པར་བྱ་ and so on, is affixed for other thing, examples of which are བསྒྲུབ་བྱ། བསྒྲུབ་པར་བྱ་བ། བསྒྲུབ་བྱའི་ལྷ། བཅག་བྱ། བཅག་པར་བྱ། བཅག་བྱའི་རྡོ།. Then the text says:

> Neutral two ག་ and ད་ are affixed

Prefix neutral ག་ and ད་ both are affixed for three meanings: self thing, other thing, and present tense.

First, the affixation for self thing. The text says:

> In གཅོད་པ་པོ་ and གཅོད་པར་བྱེད་,
> And གཅོད་པར་འགྱུར་ and དགྲི་བ་པོ་,
> And དགྲི་བར་བྱེད་ and དགྲི་བར་འགྱུར་,
> And so on to mean self thing and …

It is understood to mean the distinguishing mark of self thing, as in ཤིང་གཅོད་པ་པོ། གཅོད་བྱེད། གཅོད་པར་བྱེད། གཅོད་པར་འགྱུར་རོ། སྨྲལ་མ་དགྲི་བ་པོ། དགྲི་བར་བྱེད། དགྲི་བར་འགྱུར། གསོད་པ་པོ། གསོད་པར་བྱེད། རྒྱ་མཚོ་དཀྲུག་པ་པོ། དཀྲུག་པར་བྱེད།.

Second, the text continues:

> In གཅད་བྱའི་ཤིང་ and གཅད་པར་བྱ་,
> And དགྲི་བྱའི་སྨྲལ་མ་དགྲི་བར་བྱ་,
> And so on to mean other thing and …

The two neutrals ག་ and ད་ in གཅད་བྱའི་ཤིང་, and so on are affixed for the meaning of other thing as in གསད་བྱ། གསད་པར་བྱ་བ། གསད་བྱའི་ལུག དགག་བྱ། དགག་པར་བྱ་བ། དགག་བྱའི་སྒྲུན།.

Third, the text continues:

> In གཅོད་བཞིན་པ་ and དགྲི་བཞིན་པ་
> And so on, to produce the present.

The two neutrals ག་ and ད་ are affixed for the present where the action of agent in actual relationship with other is being done[57]. They are affixed to make the present where the verb's term is

[57] This means "is being done in the continuous present tense".

modified by a phrase assistive[58], as in ཤིང་གཅོད་བཞིན་པ། གཅོད་ཀྱིན་འདུག སྣུལ་མ་དཀྲི་བཞིན་པ། དཀྲི་ཡིན་འདུག །དོན་གཉེར་བཞིན་པ། གཉེར་གྱིན་འདུག །ཞོ་དཀྲོག་བཞིན་པ། དཀྲོག་པའི་སྐད་ཡིན།.

Female letter འ་ is affixed for four meanings: self thing; self as complement; present tense; and future. First, for the self thing, the text says:

> Female letter འ་ is affixed in འཆད་པ་པོ་,
> And འཆད་པར་བྱེད་ and འཆད་པར་འགྱུར་,
> And so on for thing of self thing and …

These—ཆོས་འཆད་པ་པོ། འཆད་པར་བྱེད། འཆད་པར་འགྱུར། མདུད་པ་འགྲོལ་བ་པོ། འགྲོལ་བྱེད། འགྲོལ་བར་འགྱུར།—and so on are self thing; it is affixed in order to make that.

Second, for the self as complement, the text says:

> In འགྲོ་བ་པོ་ and འགྲོ་བར་བྱེད་
> And so on for the meaning of self as complement
>   and …

The female letter is affixed for self as complement, examples of which are གང་དུ་འགྲོ་བ་པོ། འགྲོ་བར་བྱེད། འགྲོ་བར་འགྱུར་རོ། མགོ་འཁོར་བ་པོ། འཁོར་བྱེད། ཕྱོགས་ཤར་ནས་འཆར་བ་པོ། འཆར་བྱེད། འོད་འཚེར་བ་པོ། འཚེར་བྱེད།. It is affixed in these and others like them for self as complement where the action and agent appear to be the same entity or non-transitive.

---

[58] For phrase assistive, see the glossary. A phrase assistive is similar in function to a phrase linker. Phrase assistives are explained at length in volume one of the standard references to Tibetan grammar mentioned in the introduction. In the examples given, the phrase assistives are བཞིན་པ་ ཀྱིན་ ཡིན་ གྱིན་ all of which give the sense of a continuous action in the present.

Third, for the present tense, the text says:

> In འཁྱིལ་ལོ་ and so on for the present …

It is affixed as in ཆུ་འཁྱིལ་ལོ། འཁྱིལ་བཞིན་པ། གདན་ལ་འཁོད་བཞིན་པ། འཁོད་མུས་ཡིན། མེ་འབར་བཞིན་པ། བདེ་བར་འཚོ་བཞིན་པ། and so on, in order to produce the present tense not included by the distinction into self-other.

Fourth, for the future tense, the text says:

> And in འཁྱིལ་བར་འགྱུར་ and so on for the future.

It is affixed as in ཆུ་འཁྱིལ་བར་འགྱུར། སྨན་འཛུ་བར་འགྱུར། ལུས་འཚོ་བར་འགྱུར། and so on, in order to produce the intransitive future that is, an action that will happen where the action and agent appear not to be different, that is, intransitive.

The text says:

> The extremely female letter མ་
> Is affixed equally for self, other, and the three tenses.

The prefix extremely female མ་ letter is affixed equally for both self and other and the three tenses that is, for everything. To add to that, it is affixed for self as in མཁྱེན་པ་པོ། མཁས་པར་བྱེད།; for other as in མཁས་བྱ། མཆོད་བྱ། མཆོད་པར་བྱ།; for the past tense as in མཁྱེན་ཏོ། མཁས་པར་བྱས། མགུ་བར་བྱས།; for the present tense as in མཁྱེན་བཞིན་པ། མཛལ་བཞིན་པ། མཐུན་གྱིན་འདུག; and for the future tense as in མཁས་པར་འགྱུར། མཛའ་བར་འགྱུར། མཐུན་པར་འགྱུར།. That is, it is used equally for all of those.

The text says:

> Nonetheless, for the past of an agent in actual
> Relationship with other, the འ་ prefix

> Certainly not and ག་ and ད་ a little.

This is saying, "Nonetheless, it is certain that the འ་ prefix is never affixed for past forms of agent in actual relationship with other, and not only that but that both ག་ and ད་ also are affixed only a little".

The text says:

> For the present, the prefix བ་
> A little and for headed present
> Not having བ་ fronted is simply certain.

This is saying, "Present forms have the བ་ letter prefix only a little and not only that but also for present forms with ར་, ལ་, or ས་ heads it is simply certain that they do not have a བ་ fronted to them."

The text says:

> Furthermore, for བ་ fronted forms usually
> The agent is included in the present and
> The place of action in the future, thus …

Furthermore, བ་ fronted forms usually incorporate, of the two agent and place of action, the agent in the present and the place of action in the future. Thus, this makes a division into four of past tense, present tense, future tense, and the imperative form.

For the first, the text says:

> The past has བ་ fronting and a re-suffix …

Headed, past-form words have prefixes—བ་ and so on—and re-suffixes both affixed on them, for example, as in ལྷ་བསྒྲིམས།.

For the second, the text says:

> The present has neither of the two …Present forms have neither prefix nor re-suffix at all, for example སྒྲུབ་པ་པོ། སྒྲུབ་བྱེད། སྒྲུབ་པར་བྱེད། སྒྲུབ་པོ།.

For the third, the text says:

> The future has a fronting and no re-suffix, and …

Future forms have a fronting and do not have a re-suffix, for example, བསྒྲུབ་བྱ། བསྒྲུབ་པར་བྱ། བསྒྲུབ་བྱའི་ལྷ།.

For the fourth, imperative forms both have and do not have re-suffixes. First, in the case of having a re-suffix, the text says:

> The imperative has no fronting and has a re-suffix.

There are imperative forms without a fronting prefix and with a re-suffix, for example སྒྲུབས་ཤིག "Practise!" and སྲུངས་ཤིག "Protect it!".

Second, in the case of not having a re-suffix, the text says:

> Sometimes past and imperative having
> A bare ས་ connected to them is also acceptable.

Past and imperative word-forms usually get a re-suffix, however, sometimes both past and imperative can have a bare ས་ connected which is also acceptable, that is, allowable. Past word forms for which the connection of a bare ས་ is acceptable are as in བྱས། འདས། བལྟས། and imperative forms as in གྱིས་ཤིག ལྟོས་ཤིག སྐུས།.

4. The explanation of the divisions of the gender signs of the suffixes

The text says:

> Of the ten suffix letters,
> The four ག་, ད་, བ་ and ས་ are male,
> The three ང་, མ་, and འ་ are female,
> And the three ན་, ར་, and ལ་ are neutral;
> They affix to all name-base letters.

This is saying, "The ten suffixes as mentioned in "ག་, ང་, ད་, ན་, བ་, མ་, འ་, ར་, ལ་, and ས་ are the ten suffixes" fall into three subdivisions. What are the three? They are male, female, and neutral. First, the four ག་, ད་, བ་ and ས་ are male letters. Second, the three ང་, མ་, and འ་ are female letters. Third, the three ན་, ར་, and ལ་ are neutral letters. They, all of them, affix to all name-base letters."

5. The explanation of how the gender signs of the suffixes affix

The text says:

> How they affix has two parts:

There are two parts to the way in which suffixes affix: the way that they are affixed in relation to sound; and the way that they are affixed in relation to meaning.

5.A. The explanation of how the gender signs of the suffixes affix in relation to sound

The text says:

> First, the way of affixation in relation to sound.

For the three male suffixes, no matter which name-base letter they are affixed to, a vocalization of stronger sound is used. For the two females, a weaker sound is used. For the three neutrals an intermediate, that is, moderate sound is used.

The males in addition have the three sub-divisions of: "strongest being" which refers to the ones of stronger sound effort; "middling being" which refers to the intermediate ones slightly weaker than that; and "weakest being" which refers to the ones weaker again, the extremely weak ones. The first of those categories is this:

> The male ག་ letter having a re-suffix
> Is the strongest being; …

If the suffix male ག་ letter has a re-suffix ས་ in place, has the strongest being, for example མདོ་བཀླགས། དོན་གཟིགས།.

The text says:

> … male letter བ་
> Having a re-suffix is a middling being;

Male letter བ་ with a re-suffix connected has a middling being for example སྐྱབས། བསྐྱབས། སྐྱོབས།. Then the text says:

> And endings ག་ and བ་ without re-suffix

> Or with an ending of ད་ or ས་ are the weakest.

Name-bases having the endings of the two letters ག་ and བ་ without re-suffix and those having the endings of ད་ and ས་ , that is, having ད་ or ས་ suffixed to them, have the least being, e.g., བདག། མཆོག། ཁབ། རབ། ཡོད། བསྐྱོད། སྐྱེས། བཞེས།.

The text says:

> The strong males also are divided into
> Three sub-divisions of stronger, weaker, and
> intermediate.

The stronger male letters also divide into three sub-divisions as in the immediately preceding explanation: stronger ones are greatest being; intermediate ones, middling being; and weaker ones, weakest being.

The text says:

> Similarly, the weak females also are divided into
> The two sub-divisions of stronger and weaker;

Similar to the sub-division of males into three beings, the weaker females also are divided into the two sub-divisions of stronger female and weaker extremely female.

> ང་ and མ་ with re-suffix are female and ...

The letters ང་ and མ་ both having a re-suffix are the stronger one, the female itself, for example as in བཞེངས། གངས། དབྱིངས། བྱམས། བསྒོམས། ཉམས།. And secondly,

> ང་ and མ་ without re-suffix or
> With འ་ ending are extremely female.

The three suffix endings of ང་ and མ་ without re-suffix and of འ་ are extremely female, examples of which are: མཐོང་། ཞིང་། གསུམ། གཏམ། བཀའ། དགའ། མཁའ། མདའ།.

The text says:

> Intermediate neutral ན་, ར་ and ལ་,
> Affixed at the end of a name-base male letter
> Whether there is a re-suffix or not, and
> Affixed after a neutral name-base
> When there is a re-suffix,
> Are in contact with stronger, so change to stronger.

The intermediate vocalization of the three neutrals ན་, ར་ and ལ་, when they are affixed at the end of a name-base male letter whether they have a re-suffix on them or not, and when they are affixed after a neutral name-base together with a re-suffix, is in contact with a stronger vocalization, so it changes to stronger. For example, when in contact with a male letter name-base as in ཀུན། དཀོན། བཀར། བཀོལ། སྐྱུལ། ཅན། གཅེརད། བཅོལད། གཏན། བསྟནད། དཔོན། སྤར། དཔལ། སྤེལད། བརྩོན། བཙོརད། སྨུལད།, and so on, and affixed after a neutral name-base together with re-suffix, as in འཕོནད། ཆརད། ཐརད། ཕུལད། ཚོརད།, they are in contact with stronger, so they change to stronger. Situ and Ngul[59] differ a little on this point.

The text says:

> Affixed after a name-base female letter
> When there is no re-suffix,
> They are in contact with weaker, so change to weaker.

---

[59]... Situ Chokyi Jungnay and Ngulchu Dharmabhadra ...

The three ན་, ར་ and ལ་ when affixed after a name-base female letter and without a re-suffix, have come into contact with weaker, so they change to weaker. For example, འགྲན། འགོར། མགུལ། ལྡོན། འཛུར། མཛལ། དོན། འབར། འཛུལ། གཞོན། བྱུར། འོལ། གཡོན། བཞོར། གསལ།, and so on.

The text says:

> Those two are changeable neutral.

The above two, stronger and weaker, are changeable neutral. The meaning of "changeable" is that if they come into contact with a stronger name-base, they change to stronger and if a weaker one, they change to weaker, so, not maintaining their own form, they are spoken of as "changeable".

The text says:

> Affixed after a name-base female letter
> When there is a re-suffix,
> Because they have both stronger and weaker factors,
> They are known as "dual-character neutral".

The three ན་, ར་ and ལ་ when affixed after a female name-base letter and with a re-suffix, because of having both stronger and weaker portions, are known as "dual-character neutral". For example in བསྒྲརད། བཀྲལད། འཛལད། དོནད། དབེནད། འཛོརད། བཞརད། བྱེནད། བྱུརད། འོནད། གཡུལད། ཤརད། གསོལད།, they are in contact with a female name-base letter so have a female portion and are in contact with a re-suffix male letter so have a male portion thus they have both characters, and since the suffixes themselves are neutral, they are spoken of as "dual-character neutral".

The text says:

> Affixed after a name-base neutral name-base
> When there is no re-suffix,
> There is no change at all to stronger or weaker,
> So they are asserted to be "characterless neutral".

When affixed after the five neutral name-bases ཁ་, ཆ་, ཐ་, ཕ་, and ཚ་ without a re-suffix, there are no changes at all to stronger or weaker. For example, in མཁན། འཁོར། ཁལ། ཆེན། འཆར། འཆལ། མཐུན། ཐུར། འཐོལ། ཕན། འཕུར། འཕེལ། ཚོན། ཚུར། འཚོལ།, since both name-base and suffix are neutral and since there is no male or female gender whatsoever, they are held to be "characterless neutral".

5.B. The explanation of how the gender signs of the suffixes affix in relation to meaning

The text says:

> Second, meaning, has two parts of which …

The second one, the explanation of affixation in relation to meaning, has two parts: an explanation of how the prior one will change and of how the subsequent one will change.

First, for the explanation of how the prior one changes, the text says:

> How the prior one will change is concerned with
> What the name to which the suffix is joined
> Will come to show—self-other, and so on …

The names[60] themselves that the suffixes are affixed to have become, in dependence on their name-endings, the prior one. What the prior one shows of the various things of self-other, and so on is as follows. The text says:

> Which will usually be known through
> The capacity of the prefix joined to that name.

The meaning that the name shows normally has to be comprehended as self-other, one of the three tenses, etcetera, whatever it is, through the capacity of whichever of the five prefixes it has had connected to it. For example, the appropriate one of the four male suffixes affixed to the past tense is as in བསྒྲིགས། བསྒྲུབས། བཀག བཏབ། བཤད། བརྡས།; and affixed to self as in འགྲིགས་བྱེད། འདེབས་བྱེད། འགོག་བྱེད། སྒྲུབ་བྱེད། སྤྱད་བྱེད། མཛེས་བྱེད།; and with other as in གདགས་བྱ། དགག་བྱ། བསྒྲུབ་བྱ། བརྗོད་བྱ།; and affixed to the present tense that does not include the distinction of self-other as in འཕགས་བཞིན་པ། འཇུག་བཞིན་པ། འགྲུབ་བཞིན་པ། འཁོད་བཞིན་པ། དགྲེས་བཞིན་པ།; and with the future tense as in འབྱིང་པར་འགྱུར། འཐིབ་པར་འགྱུར། གཞུག་པར་འགྱུར། འཐོབ་པར་འགྱུར། འཆད་པར་འགྱུར།; and then, following that illustration, the two female and three neutral suffixes should also be known.

There is merely the name alone as in གདུགས། སྟོབས། བདག གཡབ། ཚོད། དུས། and imperative forms as in ཞུགས་ཤིག སྒྲུབས་ཤིག and then there is the same kind of thing, which comes in addition to the principal statement above of dependence on the prefix, that it is also necessary to understand the situation of no prefix but capacity to show self-other, and so on, as above, for example in རྟོགས་བྱེད། རྟོགས་ཟིན། རྩོམ་བྱེད། གླེང་བྱ། སྐོར་

[60] Name(s) throughout this text means "grammatical name(s)". For grammatical names, see the glossary.

བཞིན་པ། སྔོན་པར་འགྱུར། སྐྱོབས་ཤིག བྱས། and that of the ད་ and ས་ re-suffixes in themselves showing the past, for example as in གྱུརད། འདས། བྱས། གྲགས།.

Except for the examples in the last paragraph of three affixations of ས་ producing the past and the special case of its definitely not being affixed onto an འ་ of the past, it should be understood that on other recipients with whatever meaning of self-other, etcetera, that meaning can be changed by phrase assistives.

Second, for the explanation of how the subsequent one will be changed:

> How the subsequent one will be changed is as follows.

How the name-endings of the subsequent ones change is dictated by the individual cases and divides up into four ways as follows.

First, the text says:

> Male suffix draws another male at the end of the
> name ...

The gender of the suffix at the end of that earlier name, if the name must have an ending connected that will be a new part of that name itself, uses the majority case of drawing concordant gender and hence draws a male name-ending of a male name-base to a male suffix. For example as in, རྟོག་པ། དཔྱིད་ཀ། ཐད་ཀ། གཉིས་ཀ། མཁྱེནད་པ། འབྱོརད་པ། དགོངས་པ།.

Second, the text says:

> Female draws a female at the end of the name ...

As above, where a male suffix drew a male name-ending, a female one will draw a female name-ending, for example as in གསིང་མ། ཐམ་པ། སྙིང་པ། དགའ་བ།.

Third, the text says:

> And neutral draws a neutral.

A neutral suffix will draw a neutral name-base, for example, དགུན་ཁ། དབྱར་ཁ། སྟར་ཁ། འཕལ་ཁ། གསལ་ཁ།. Then the text says:

> Those ways are the ways of equivalent gender sign being drawn.

This is saying, "The above are the ways of drawing equivalent gender of suffix and name-base genders".

Fourth, the text says:

> There are also very many cases of ease-of-expression being drawn.

The primary one is that way of drawing it so that it is concordant with the name-ending and then there are the ways of drawing it so that it makes for ease-of-expression of the dhatu[61], of having to conform with the ways of the world, and so on which also

---

[61] Dhatu here is a Sanskrit grammatical term meaning the root which, after morphological change, becomes a word. The same term exists in Tibetan grammar is "byings", though Tibetan language does not actually have roots that undergo morphological change. The term is being used very loosely here—it simply means the basic grammatical name before the letter is added, which, correctly referred to, is not a dhatu. This matter is explained extensively in volume one of the standard references to Tibetan grammar mentioned in the introduction.

appear very frequently. The latter ones also must be comprehended without getting the particulars tangled. For example, male drawing female as in ཐོག་མ།, female drawing male as in ཁང་པ་, neutral drawing female as in ཐལ་མོ།, neutral drawing male as in ཚར་པ།, and many others occur. Not only must they be understood, but there is old orthography[62] as well where there are very many cases of bringing equivalent gender but which most editors of the new language revisions state to be an outdated system. For example, the cases in old orthography of drawing matching gender such as བྲག་ཅ། and དཀོན་ཅོག་རིན་ཅེན། are written in new orthography as བྲག་ཆ། and དཀོན་མཆོག་རིན་ཆེན། and it is a key point that these also have to be understood.

The way of drawing for ease-of-expression does not result in concordance of gender rather, it is done chiefly for ease-of-expression, hence it results in concordance of term. Thus, this appears in both *The Thirty* and *Gender Signs* as their directly stated intent[63].

The text says:

> Furthermore these items at the end of a name—

---

[62] Tibetan language went through three revisions after Thumi Saṃbhoṭa made the original definitions. In one of them, there were changes to the rules for spelling. This resulted in terms written in old and new ways, that is, in old and new orthographies. This matter is explained extensively in volume one of the standard references to Tibetan grammar mentioned in the introduction.

[63] Meaning that you can find both ways of drawing terms actually written down in both the treatises, meaning that they both explicitly show that these were intended by Thumi himself and are not a later invention.

> The eight cases, the concluders, and so on
> With their equivalence of gender or their harmony of
> sound—
> Are drawn according to the force of the prior one.

This is saying, "Following on from the above explanation of the ways of drawing the name-ending, and so on, which is now finished, there is the way of drawing the cases and phrase linkers[64], which is as follows. The just-explained name-endings draw, by the force of the prior part's suffix, the cases, and so on in a process either of mutually-equivalent gender or ease-of-expression's concordance of term. These name-endings drawn like this are in fact the eight cases—case one, just expressing the entity of dharmas; case two, the objective term; case three, agentive term; case four, purpose and need; case five, source term; case six, connective term; case seven, basis; case eight, calling term—and they are the concluders and the others explicitly laid out in the body of the text[65]—continuative; separation and inclusion; emphasis; owner term; phrase ornament; timing; and so on. And all of them have to conform to the process that the subsequent one is brought in concordance with the force of the prior name."

The text says:

> The particular division of what has been placed—
> Either a "case" or "linker"—can be known from the
> name equivalents resulting from
> The connection at the end of that name or phrase.

---

[64] For phrase linker, see the glossary. Phrase linkers are explained at length in volume one of the standard references to Tibetan grammar mentioned in the introduction.

[65] … in Thumi's root text, *The Thirty Verses* …

This is saying, "These just-explained sub-divisions of what is affixed and where it is affixed are to be properly known from the name equivalents[66] coming beyond, that is, the ones that will be connected to the ends of the phrases[67], that is, the names together with the cases or other non-case phrase linkers.[68]"

The text says:

> To explain further, case one expresses
> Just the entity of the thing;
> Its signifiers, for example like "pot" and "pillar",
> Are few in the Tibetan language.

This is saying, "Further to what was just explained, case one is the expression of just the entity of the thing. Its signifying terms, for example like བུམ་པ་ "pot", ཀ་བ་ "pillar", and ལྷ་ "god", and so on, are themselves the expressors of just the entity of the thing, but in the language of the Snowy Land of Tibet, there are very few of them.[69]"

---

[66] For name equivalents, see the glossary.

[67] Phrase(s) throughout this text means "grammatical phrase(s)". For grammatical phrase, see the glossary.

[68] A case is actually the term which indicates a case, so case here refers to the particular terms that are markers of cases. "Linker" is short for phrase linker; for phrase linker, see the glossary.

[69] Grammatical names are similar to but not the same as nouns of the English language. Whereas languages like Sanskrit and English have a very large array of naming words, like nouns, the Tibetan language has very few. This matter is dealt with extensively in volume one of the standard references to Tibetan grammar mentioned in the introduction.

The text says:

> Karma and place of action mean the same;
> Showing that some place of an action like that,
> Has had an action done to it,
> Is the second, the objective case and
> The second's sub-division, identity.
> It is like the fourth, purposiveness's three but for
> A place of action that has had an action done to it
> Where that or what is connected with it
> Is not benefited, that is the second,
> For example, like "going to the east".

"Karma" and "place of action" mean the same[70] and given that, the showing that a place of action has had an action done to it appears as the second case[71], "objective case", and the internal division of the second case, "identity". Moreover, it does indeed appears to be the same as the fourth case, purpose and need's three[72], but the thing that distinguishes them is that, if there is no benefit to that place of action that has had an action done to it or to the thing connected with it, then it is the second case, objective, for example, "going to the east".

The text says:

> If there is benefit, it is the fourth,

---

[70] … as was explained earlier …

[71] The second case has only the two parts: the karma (one) being the place where an action (two) is done, for example, "going down a road". There is no agent acting on the karma in this case.

[72] The fourth case involves someone (one) doing something on account of or for (two) someone or something else (three). For example, he gave grass to the horse.

> For example, like "giving to a beggar".

If there is benefit for that place of action that has had an action done to it or to the karma connected with it, it is the fourth case, "purpose and need", for example, དགེ་སློང་ལ་སྦྱིན། "giving to a monk", སློང་མཁན་ལ་སྟེར། "giving to a beggar", ཞིང་དུ་ཆུ་འདྲེན་, "bringing water to a field".

The text says:

> Even if there is no benefit, if the place of action
> And the action are of the same entity,
> It is the second's sub-division, identity,
> For example, like "appeared as the deity".

Even if there is no benefit to that place of action that has had an action done to it, if both the place of action and the action are of the same entity, then it is the second case's internal division, "identity", for example, ལྷ་རུ་གསལ། "(he himself) appeared as the deity", འོད་དུ་འཚེར། "(a light) radiating light".

The text says:

> If there is just the meaning of something which is
> relying on
> Or is positioned on or existing on something else
> And otherwise does no specific action,
> It is the seventh case, basis,
> For example, like "there is a man on top".

If it just shows the meaning of something that relies on or is positioned on or exists on something else and other than that does no specific action then it is the seventh case, basis, for example as in སྟེང་དུ་མི་ཡོད། "there is a man on top" and དབུས་སུ་ཇོ་བོ་བཞུགས། "the lord stayed in Central Tibet".

The text says:

> If it is like the meaning of the second's time-
> circumstance,
> It is the seventh's sub-division of time-circumstance,
> For example, "When the Magha moon appears,
> The commemoration of miracles is undertaken".

If it has the sort of meaning of the two things of time and circumstance, then it is the seventh case's internal division, time-circumstance, for example, ཧོར་ཟླ་དང་པོ་ཤར་བ་ན་ཆོ་འཕྲུལ་དུས་ཆེན་ཚུགས། "When the moon of the first lunar month appears, the commemoration of miracles is undertaken"[73].

The text says:

> The terms which elicit cases two, four,
> Seven, and time-circumstance and identity
> Are སུ་, ར་, རུ་, དུ་, ན་, ལ་, and ཏུ་,
> And given that they usually agree with the ལ་ term
> They are also called "the la-equivalent cases".

The terms which elicit these five—cases two, four, and seven and the second's internal division, identity, and the seventh's internal division, time-circumstance—are these seven: སུ་, ར་, རུ་, དུ་, ན་, ལ་, and ཏུ་. They usually concur with the way of placing the ལ་ term, so they are also called the "la-equivalents", and, when they have become phrase assistives and hence turned into cases, they are also called "la-equivalent cases".

---

[73] This is one of the eight great commemorations of Śhākyamuni Buddha's activities. It commemorates the forty days during which he showed great miracles. The Magha moon means the moon when it is in the house of the constellation named "Magha" in Indian astrology.

The system of their agreeing with the way of its affixation[74] means that they are in agreement or equivalent as in དབུས་སུ་འགྲོ། and དབུས་ལ་འགྲོ།[75] being equivalent.

The text says:

> Nevertheless, it says in the *Speech Door*
> That ན་ and ལ་ are not placed for identity.

Despite that, the *Speech Door*[76] says that both ན་ and ལ་ are not used for case two's internal division, identity:

> དུ་, and so on concur with ལ་;
> The two for identity are special.

Here it also has to be pointed out that "usually" is a word of uncertainty, for example, it means that constructions like ཟླ་ན་གསལ། and འོད་ལ་འཚེར།[77] are not all right.

The text says:

---

[74] ... that is, with the way of the affixation of ལ་ itself, the name-sake of the la-equivalents ...

[75] Both have exactly the same meaning "going to the central parts" because the la-equivalent in the second sentence performs all the actions of the six other equivalents, including of the སུ་ in the first sentence.

[76] The name of a grammar text written in the middle eleventh century C.E. which is regarded as a particularly excellent exposition of Tibetan grammar. Situ Rinpoche cited it frequently in his *Great Commentary*, often taking it as a basis for his own arguments. See Speech Door Weapon in the glossary.

[77] Compare these with the correctly done examples a page or so earlier.

> If the place to which a case is connected
> Does an action somewhere far or near,
> It is the third one, the agentive case,
> For example, "I explained".

If the place to which the case is connected does an action somewhere, no matter whether it is nearby or far away[78], then it is the third case, the agentive term, for example བདག་གིས་བཤད། "I explained" and མིག་གིས་ལྟ་ "He (his eye) looked" are cases of[79] the verb being nearby and མིག་གིས་ཤེལ་རྩེའི་རྩེ་མོ་ནས་ཕྱོགས་ཐམས་ཅད་དུ་ཡང་ཡང་དུ་ལེགས་པར་བལྟས་སོ། "Pointing the telescope in every direction he looked carefully again and again" is a case of its being far away.

The text says:

> If it definitely does no action and
> Shows just the making of a connection between former
> and later,
> It is the sixth case, connective term,
> For example, like "my eye".

Without the specific doing of an action to a karma, that is, a place of action, if it shows just the making of a connection between former and later words, then it is the sixth case, named "the connective term", for example as in བདག་གི་མིག "my eye", ཁབ་ཀྱི་རྩེ། "the point of the needle".

The text says:

> The terms which elicit the third and sixth cases

---

[78] The verb denoting the action is located …

[79] This means that it does not matter whether the verb of a transitive action is close to or many words away from the agentive case marker.

> Are the five གི་, ཀྱི་, གྱི་, འི་, and ཡི་,
> With and without a ས་ ending respectively.

This is saying, "The terms which elicit both the sixth and third cases are those with a sa at the end of the word གིས་, ཀྱིས་, གྱིས་, འིས་, and ཡིས་ and those without a ས་ at the end of the word, the five གི་, ཀྱི་, གྱི་, འི་, and ཡི་".

The text says:

> If it has the meaning of something that arises from or
> Comes out or issues forth from somewhere,
> It is the fifth case, source;
> For example, "heard from the mouth".
> The terms which elicit it are ནས་ and ལས་.
> Segregation and inclusion also are included in the fifth.

If it has the meaning of something that arises from, comes out of, or issues from some thing which is a basis, it is the fifth case, named "source", for example ཞལ་ནས་ལེགས་པར་བཤད་ཐོས། "heard a good explanation from the mouth (in person)", རྒྱ་མཚོ་ནས་ནོར་བུ་འབྱུང་ "jewels come from the ocean". The terms which elicit it are the two, ནས་ and ལས་. And not only that, but both segregation and inclusion also are included in the fifth case, for example, segregation as in ལྷ་ཡི་ནང་ནས་བརྒྱ་སྦྱིན་མཆོག་ "from amongst the gods, Kaushika is supreme" and inclusion as in སྤྱི་གཙུག་ནས་རྐང་མཐིལ་བར་ "from the top of the crown to the soles of the feet".

The text says:

> Furthermore, if the meanings of phrase equivalents
> Before and after are to be included,
> དང་, ཀྱང་, ཡང་, and འང་, and so on are connected.

Furthermore, if there is to be inclusion of the meanings of whatever words before and after, the terms of inclusion དང་ and ཀྱང་ and ཡང་ and འང་ and so on must be connected, for example, ལྷ་དང་མི་དང་ལྷ་མ་ཡིན་དང་དྲི་ཟར་བཅས་པའི་འཇིག་རྟེན་ཡི་རངས་ཏེ་ "The world of gods and men and demi-gods and gandharvas rejoiced", བསད་ཀྱང་ལངས། "woke and rose", མགོ་ཡང་གུག་སྐྲ་འང་དཀར། "head and curly hair too, were white".

The text says:

> If several enumerations repeat the meaning,
> The separation-inclusion terms are affixed.

If many similar terms supporting the meaning is needed, then the terms of separation or inclusion are affixed prior to each. For example: where the meaning is supported འཆི་མེད་དམ། ཉམ་སད་དམ། མིག་མི་འཛུམ་ "deathless, always awake, and eyes not closing"; and where the words are supported པདྨ་དཀར་པོའམ། པདྨ་དཀར་པོ་ལྟ་བུའི་སེམས་དཔའ། "white lotus or brave-minded like a white lotus"; and where both word and meaning are supported བསྐོར་ཞིང་བསྐོར་ཞིང་སླར་ཡང་དེ་རུ་འབབ། "turning and turning and once again falling down there".

The text says:

> If there are the meanings of negation or
> Of owner, then one of the gender signs of the པ་
>   section
> From beginning to end as appropriate is affixed.

The མ་ letter found within the པ་ section when affixed before, after, or in between—any of these three—shows negation or is the term of negation as in མ་ཡིན། མི་འདུག བདག་མིན། འདི་མེད། མི་སྒྲུ་མ་ཡིན། ག་མ་ས།. And, the པ་ and བ་ and མ་ found within the པ་ section—that is, the male, female, and neutral genders, whichever is appropriate when showing the term of the owner—are, if affixed at the end of the name-base, the distinguish ers of the meaning of the owner, for example རྟ་པ་ "horseman", ནང་པ་, insider (male), ལྷ་རྩེ་བ་ "person at the peak of the gods (neutral, meaning both male and female are included)".

The text says:

> Phrase linkers that become ornaments also
> Are connected if there is a follow-up to their meaning.

The phrase linkers that are also ornaments must be connected only in a position with a meaning trailing them, that is, if a meaning is connected following them, for example མཛེས་ཀྱང་མཛེས། "more beautiful than beautiful", བཏུད་ཀྱང་ཁྲོ་ "bowing but angry". And, it is not acceptable to connect them when that condition is not fulfilled.

The text says:

> Likewise, if there is more to be shown,
> A continuative term is connected.

Similar to the way of connecting phrase ornaments just explained, if there is something more or further to be shown, the continuative term must be connected, for example, དོན་རྟོགས་ཏེ་ཉམས་སུ་བླངས། "realized the meaning, that is, gained the experience (in meditation)". Then the text says:

> When a phrase equivalent is complete,
> The concluder terms are connected.

When a phrase equivalent is a complete expression[13], one of the concluder terms must be connected. For example, མཆོག་གོ།, བཟང་ངོ།.

6. Teaching the need for the suffixes

The text says:

> Why do they need to be affixed?
> If it is not associated with a female letter, a vowel,
> Then a male letter, a consonant, cannot be expressed.

This is saying, "If you ask, "Why do the suffix letters need to be affixed?", the answer is that it is because if the male letters, the consonants, do not have a female letter, a vowel, then they cannot be expressed."

The text says:

> Therefore, it is convenient to assert five vowels.
> Moreover, for such male letters having a vowel,
> If it does not have one of the ten suffixes affixed, then

---

[13] Similar to the idea of having an English expression which is a complete thought and needing to end it with a full stop, in Tibetan grammar one has a phrase equivalent which has arrived at being a complete expression and, in order to show the conclusion of that complete expression, a concluder term must be added to it. In the example given here, the ངོ་ at the end of the expression མཆོག་གོ།, བཟང་ངོ། is the concluder. All of the cases, phrase linkers, phrase assistives, and so on are extensively explained in volume one of the standard references to Tibetan grammar mentioned in the introduction.

The meaning carried by the names which show just the entity[14], and
The distinctions of the names' meaning shown by the phrases, and
The verbal expressions that convey such meanings would not exist.
It is so, because names are drawn out from the letters,
Phrases are drawn out from the names,
And by phrases, the meanings are shown.

This is saying, "For that reason, it is convenient to accept the four vowels actually taught together with the implied ཨ་ to make five[15]. Not only that, but for those male letters ཀ་, and so on, having a vowel that is, the gigu and so on, also, if they do not have any—whatever it might—of the ten suffix letters, in place[16], then the meanings which are the names that show the entity, the distinctions of the meanings which are the phrases that show them, and the expressions of speech that have the meaning to be expressed, would not exist at all. It is so, because the names are drawn out from, that is, come from, the letters; the phrases are drawn out

---

[14] Grammatical names only show a thing, that is, they are like nouns which merely nominate a thing or entity.

[15] The issue of whether there are four or five vowels in the Tibetan language is one of the great, unresolved arguments amongst Tibetan grammarians.

[16] In Tibetan grammar, name-base must have a suffix letter attached to it, therefore, the ten suffix letters are crucial to the production of the language. Without their application, the words of the language literally cannot be made.

from the names, and it is by way of the phrases that the meanings can be individually shown without mix-up."[17]

The text says:

> If there were no names, phrases, or expressions,
> The teaching of ordinary and extraordinary
> Knowables also would become non-existent.

This is saying, "If there were no names, phrases, or expressions, then the showing of the knowables which are the meanings in the treatises both of the ordinary outsider's Vedas with their poetry, and so on and of the extraordinary sūtras and tantras of the sage, the bhagavat buddha—as seen in the *Translated Word* and *Translated Treatises*—also would become non-existent"[18].

The text says:

---

[17] This is a very important section of this text. It reflects a section of the *Application of Gender Signs* that shows how Tibetan language is structured. The structure of Tibetan language is that letters make grammatical names and they also make phrase linkers. When phrase linkers are added to grammatical names, grammatical phrases result. Grammatical nouns and phrases together make up expressions. This structure is very different from English and understanding it is one of the keys to understanding Tibetan language. This matter is dealt with extensively in volume one of the standard references to Tibetan grammar mentioned in the introduction.

[18] If there were no grammatical names, grammatical phrases, and resulting expressions, then the important literature of non-Buddhists such as the Hindus with their Vedic literature and of the Buddhists with their words of the Buddha and words of master who wrote treatises explaining those words, would never come to exist in the first place.

> Therefore may this, spoken following
> The Noble Land's experts[19],
> Be realized by all beings.

This is the aspiration being made with those words[20], "Therefore, since there is that need, may the intended meaning of the two treatises, *The Thirty* and *The Application of Gender Signs*, that I, Thumi, motivated by love, set forth following the great experts of the Indian Noble Land, Braḥman Livikara and others[21], be, without mistake, easily realized by all beings of the Snowy Land".

The text says:

> It seems like this is just a pile of terminology and
> words
> But an enormous meaning is distinguished within it.
> Rely on a correct understanding of language then
> Remain in seeking out without mistake what is
> meaningful!

This is saying, "Although this looks like this text is just a collection of a few terms about words, the distinctions of meaning contained in it are very great. For example, if we use one word

---

[19] The Noble Land is India and the experts referred to are the masters of Indian language with whom Thumi Saṃbhoṭa studied. Following the knowledge gained from them, Thumi Saṃbhoṭa wrote a new grammar for the Tibetan language. May the treatise *Application of Gender Signs*, which is one of the defining treatises of that new grammar, be thoroughly understood by all.

[20] This is the aspiration made by Thumi Saṃbhoṭa at the conclusion of his composition, *The Application of Gender Signs*.

[21] Braḥman Livikara and others were his Indian language teachers.

structure to demonstrate this: there are the terms གྲི་, དྲི་, and བྲི་ based on the name-base letters ག་, ད་, and བ་ respectively. This seems to be just a few words collected together but, if each is analysed, as follows, the differences in meaning are very great. Firstly, we have མཚོན་གྱི་རལ་གྲི། "the weapon sword"; སྣ་ལ་བསྣམ་བུའི་དྲི། "the snot on the handkerchief"; and རི་མོ་བྲི་ "drawing a picture". On top of that, there were the previous kings Wang and Gung who fought with each other because of a misunderstanding that arose when a scribe mistook དྲི་ snot for གྲི་ sword[22].

Therefore, for that reason, first serve at the holy friend's lotus feet and involve yourself with the grammar texts that purely show the signs of the language then, with the strength of learning produced, you will un-mistakenly differentiate names and phrases; having done that, you must hold dear, that is, cherish deep in your heart, seeking what is meaningful".[23]

The text says:

> It is well-known that the experts say that anyone who
> Is not expert whether he is ignorant to the meaning or
> not,
> Who follows this approach will be someone who

---

[22] One king got the message that his weapons were snot rather than swords because of mistake in a single letter in the spelling and that started a war between them.

[23] This is a paraphrase of the advice that Thumi Saṃbhoṭa gives in his *Thirty Verses*. First find a suitable spiritual teacher and begin by learning one's own language. When one knows that, one will be able to read and understand the meaning. Then one can leave that behind and do nothing but pursue what is truly meaningful.

> "Knowing terms has no ignorance".

This is saying, "If you are in the position of having heard and contemplated the language texts of your language like that[24], you will be able to analyse the intent contained in the Conqueror's excellent discourses[25] and the meanings of the texts containing the commentaries to his intent by the Indian and Tibetan experts and accomplished ones, and having done so, will have a fully-developed intellect free of ignorance and will become a great expert because of it. On the other hand, if you are not in the position of having heard and contemplated the language texts of your language, you will have the ignorance of not knowing the meaning of Buddha-word and commentaries on their intent and not only that but will finish up having the ignorance of not knowing the meaning even of worldly activities.

"Moreover, such ignorance and non-ignorance is produced by being expert or not in the two root texts of grammar here, *The Thirty* and *Application of Gender Signs* which in Tibet are called "Terms, The Thirty and Gender Signs" and it is also known everywhere within the writings of Indian and Tibetan learned and accomplished ones that, "If you know the terms, you are not ignorant of the meaning".

The text says:

> Anyone who has not learned the subject here and who
> is measured as being ignorant of it,

---

[24] … just mentioned.

[25] … the excellent discourses of the Buddha, corresponding in Tibetan to the *Kangyur* or *Translated Word* …

> Who enters an institution of exposition, debate, and
> composition,
> Will, like a fox in lion's clothing,
> Sooner or later be revealed.

Because it is the grandmother of all textual systems of pure signs of language, the ignorant ones who have not learned, have not trained in these *Thirty* and *Gender Signs*, enter into the institutions, the ranks where the three activities of the learned[26] are conducted, and just spout the meanings of the intent of the excellent discourses of the conqueror, debate with others, write their own texts, and so on. They are like foxes in lion's clothing—for the time being they look like lions, but one day that will change and their lack of learning will be nakedly revealed.

The text says:

> Therefore, to you who seek a clear intellect,
> I say, "Hey! Come quick and look at the image
> In this mirror that clearly displays all reflections
> Of the difficult points of the *Application of Gender*
> *Signs*!"

This is saying, "Therefore, for that reason, you of clear intellect who seek the meanings of hearing and contemplation, "Hey! I cry out, come here now, quickly!" and look at this image on the surface of this mirror in which clearly appears, un-muddled, all the reflections of the difficult points, that is, the meanings difficult to comprehend that are the greater points of the *Application of Gender Signs*.

The text says:

[26] The three are exposition, debate, and composition.

> If errors have accumulated in here,
> They are confessed right here in view of the experts.

This is saying, "If mistakes have accumulated in this *Mirror that Reveals the Difficult Points of the "Application of Gender Signs"*, they are admitted and confessed before all experts who are right here, that is, straight in front of me".

The text says:

> By the virtue obtained from this small effort,
> May all comprehend the meaning of this.

This is the dedication and aspiration. It is saying:

> Through the virtue obtained from the small effort involved in producing this text of the *Application of Gender Signs* by myself, Yangchen Drubpay Dorje, may all of the migrators in the Snowy Land nicely comprehend the meaning of it and then, via the three, exposition, debate, and, composition, may they have the means to complete the aims of themselves and others.

I would like to say this here:[27]

The *Thirty* and *Gender Signs*, the jewel wealth of our fulfilled desires and hopes,

---

[27] This is a standard formulation indicating that an author has finished his work but would like to add his own thoughts to finish up with. What follows, up to the final colophon, is in verse. And again, Yangchen Drubpay Dorje's abilities as a poet are remarkable.

That came from churning the ocean mine of Thumi's motivation[28],
Is a glorious thing seen blazing with the light of benefit and ease
That all of the previous experts have held as dear as their eyes.

Thus there are constellations of commentaries to the treatises
Emanated by the experts but at their centre is Ngulchu[29],
Whose supreme, brilliant moon of fine explanations,
Is able to open up the drooping and closed Kunda of good fortune[30].

E MA, how could the far limits of the ocean of the system of the reference texts
Of language be within the domain of the eye of intellect of the immature?
Due to that, if errors have accumulated in here,
They are confessed to the experts right before me; please wipe them off![31]

By the whiteness, like snow, a conch, the root of lotus, and a milk lake,
Of the little bit of virtue obtained from this small effort,
May the holy dharma of scripture and realization
Increase fully in the minds of self and others.

---

[28] Jewels and wealth come from the ocean, because of the connection with nāgas and their wealth.

[29] His guru, mentioned at the beginning of the text, Dharmabhadra.

[30] The white Kunda flower opens only in the moonlight and even then very rarely.

[31] The text is a mirror according to him, so it should be wiped clean by those who know better, if there are any smudges on it!

My own disciple Tshedrung Gyaltsen Chodan pressed me, saying that an easy-to-understand commentary using ordinary terms to explain *A Mirror that Reveals the Difficult Points of the "Application of Gender Signs"* was needed. From my side, I had not even an atom of confidence that I could expound such a thing, but not wanting to turn away the request of the person who prompted me, I just spouted this out. It was completed by the Kachen[32] Bhikṣhu Padma at the end of the day of the third Completion of the light phase of the Siddhartin[33].

[32] Kachen is the name of a degree from Tashi Lhunpo; like the later instituted Geshe degree of Gelugpa monastic institutes.

[33] This is the full moon of the last month of the Female Earth Sheep Year.

Glossary of Terms

This is a glossary of grammar terms used in this book. A short but clear definition of each term is given. Extensive definitions of all the Tibetan parts of speech are given in the two volumes of the standard references to Tibetan grammar mentioned in the introduction and those treatises are strongly recommended for those wanting a complete explanation of the Tibetan grammar terms.

Accounting for something else, Tib. rnam grangs gzhan can: This phrase indicates the function of what is called a pronoun in English.

Actual source, Tib. 'byung khung dngos: This is the name for the actual source case, given to distinguish it from the one sub-division that exists for the source case. See under "source case".

Agentive term, Tib. byed sgra: This is an abbreviation of "term of the agent" *q.v.*

Ali, Skt. āli: The name in Sanskrit for the vowel set. It literally means "the *string* of vowels starting with *ā*".

Bare letter, Tib. yig ge rkyang pa: A bare letter is any consonant letter of the alphabet to which another letter—either super- or sub-fix—has not been affixed. E.g., ག་ is the bare letter "ga" whereas the letter "ga" with super-fixed sa and sub-fixed ra སྒྲ་ is not a bare letter.

Beginning of a name, Tib. ming gi thog ma: This refers to the position immediately before any given grammatical name.

Bend: Tib. kyed: This is a poetic term for the ེ "drengbu" vowel sign.

Boundary of a name, Tib. ming mtshams: This refers to the position immediately after any given grammatical name.

Calling terms, Tib. bod sgra: This is an abbreviation of "term of calling" *q.v.*

Case, Tib. rnam dbye: Tibetan language has grammar cases which are very similar to English grammar cases but not the same as Tibetan cases, therefore an comprehensive effort to match the names of Tibetan cases with English ones has not been made.

Cases in Tibetan grammar, as in English grammar, show the relationship between a noun and other parts of a sentence. There are eight cases in Tibetan grammar, though sometimes the first, which is the noun itself without any further case sign added, is left out to give seven. The cases are: 1) the noun itself with no further relationship to anything else shown; 2) the objective case, also called "site of a function", meaning that shows the place where intransitive action occurs is shown; 3) the agentive case, meaning that the agent of a transitive action is shown; 4) the purposive case, also called "necessity and purpose", meaning that a relationship to some object is shown in which some need or purpose on the side of the object is shown; 5) the source case meaning that the source of something is shown; 6) the connective case, meaning that a relationship between two things is shown; 7) the locative case, also called "site of support", meaning that the place which is a basis for something is shown; and 8) the calling case, which indicates that another being is being called or hailed.

There are two sub-division cases: 1) the second case has a sub-division called "identity" and 2) the seventh case has a sub-division called "timing". According to *Situ's Words*, the first means "at the time of something being acted on and something acting, the object and action are one entity, as in 'od du 'tsher ba (radiating light)" and the second means "when they are connected to have the meaning expressing time, as in nyi ma shar ba na chos ston (teaching the dharma when the sun rises)".

Completing word, Tib. rdzogs tshig: This is one of three names for the set of phrase linkers which are used to show that a sentence has been completed. The other terms are "concluder" and "coupled concluder".

Concluder, Tib. slar bsdu: See under "completing word".

Concordant bases, Tib. mthun pa'i gzhi: This phrase is used to indicate that two items are of the same type or belong to the same category of thing.

Concordant-class segregation, Tib. mthun pa'i dgar ba: This is the name of one aspect of the subdivision of the fifth or source case *q.v.* It has a matching aspect called non-concordant-class segregation.

Connection, Tib. sbyor ba: The general name for the process in which the parts of speech are built up from letters. Letters are connected to produces the basic parts of speech—grammatical names and grammatical phrases—of the Tibetan language.

Connective term, Tib. 'brel sgra: This is an abbreviation of "term of connection" *q.v.*

Consonant, Tib. gsal byed: The Tibetan lettering set is composed of two types of letters, no more and no less: vowels and conso nants. The name for a consonant in Tibetan, gsal byed, means that the consonant "clearly produces" a sound of its own so that it can be readily distinguished from all other consonants.

Continuative, Tib. lhag bcas: This is the name of a set of three phrase linkers which, by definition, function to show that there is more to come.

Convention, Tib. tha snyad: This term is defined as meaning any verbal or mental construct which has been agreed upon as the signifier of a particular meaning. For example, "red"—both the concept and the word, whether written or spoken—is the convention used to indicate the colour red.

Coupled concluder, Tib. zla sdud: See under "completing word". This term gets its name from the fact that, as the type of term which concludes a sentence, it has its spelling matched to, so is coupled with, the preceding word.

Dependent linker, Tib. gzhan dbang gi prad: This is the name for one of the two types of phrase linker, the other being the independent linker. See under "linker" for more.

Differentiating tsheg, Tib. phyed tsheg: A letter ང་ nga followed by a ། shad stroke must have a ་ tsheg punctuation mark placed in between the letter nga and the shad. The tsheg ensures that the ང། nga shad combination is not mistaken for a letter བ ba, which it easily can be without the added tsheg. Thus, this tsheg is called a differentiating tsheg because it differentiates the nga shad combination from a ba letter.

The *Fine Explanation Great Living Tree* explains: "It is required between a final letter nga and a shad in order to prevent the possibility of that construction being mistaken for a ba letter, for example in མ་བསྒྲིབས་ཤིང་།. Other letter-shad combinations do not have a tsheg inserted in between them, for example in གཡུར་ཟ་བའི།".

Drengbu, Tib. greng bu: This is the name, literally meaning "a small swash", of the second of the four Tibetan vowels, having a sound similar to "e".

Ending, Tib. mtha': This is the general name for any letter added in either the suffix or re-suffix position to a name-base letter. In other words, it is the final or ending letter of the intertsheg under consideration.

An intertsheg by definition always has an ending letter. However, new rules that were introduced in the language revisions allowed for certain endings not to be written. Therefore, "no ending" is discussed for those cases where no apparent ending is present, even if, grammatically speaking, there is an ending letter.

A "name's ending" is the ending letter on a grammatical name.

Five prefixes, Tib. sngon 'jug lnga: The prefix letters are a set of five letters. They are derived from the set of ten suffix letters.

Five uses of inclusion, separation, reason, timing, and verbal instruction, Tib. sdud, 'byed, rgyu mtshan, tshe skabs, gdams ngag: These are the names of the five different functions defined for the དང་ dang term.

Four exhibitors of the function of the ali vowels, Tib. dbyangs bzhi'i bya ba gsal bar byed pa: There are four written signs used to indicate the function of the Tibetan vowels. Although there is a fifth vowel sound in the Tibetan language, no sign is needed to indicate it. It is the vowel "a". See also "Āli".

Forceful ending, Tib. drag mtha': The letters ད་ and ས་ can be used in the re-suffix position. In that cases, they are in the ending position of the intertsheg of which they are a part and cause the pronunciation of the intertsheg to be markedly strengthened. Therefore, they are called "forceful endings".

Forceful ད་ endings, Tib. da drag: See under forceful ending.

Forceful ས་ endings, Tib. sa drag: See under forceful ending.

Fronted, Tib. 'phul ba: This term used to indicate that an intertsheg has a prefix on it. See also "fronting".

Fronting, Tib. 'phul rten: This is the general name for all prefix letters given that they push into an intertsheg from the front.

Four vowels, Tib. dbyangs bzhi: Thumi Saṃbhoṭa states only that there are four written marks used to indicate the function of vowels. None of his remaining treatises on grammar (only two of the original eight are extant) discusses how many vowel sounds there are in the language. This has led to a great deal of debate amongst Tibetan grammarians over the centuries. In recent times, some Westerners have claimed that there is a fifth "hidden" vowel but that exceeds that the system itself says. In fact, there are five vowels sounds. However, it is a mistake to say that the fifth one is "hidden". It is not hidden but is a part of the pronunciation of consonants that does not need a written mark to indicate its presence.

Gender Signs, Tib. rtags: Tibetan grammar assigns gender to the letters of the alphabet. The genders affect pronunciation and several other aspects of the language. The system of letter gender and its application are defined in Thumi Saṃbhoṭa's treatise called *Application of Gender Signs*.

Gigu, Tib. gi gu: This is the name, literally meaning "bent over gi", of the first of the four Tibetan vowels. It has a bent over shape and having a sound similar to "i", hence its name.

Grammatical name, Tib. ming: This is a longer term for what is simply called a "name" in Tibetan grammar. The word "grammatical" has been added to make it clear that this is not a name in the usual English sense but a name in the specific Tibetan grammatical sense.

Grammatical phrase, Tib. tshig: This is a longer term for what is simply called a "phrase" in Tibetan grammar. The word "grammatical" has been added to make it clear that this is not a phrase in the usual English sense but a phrase in the specific Tibetan grammatical sense.

Hook, Tib. gug: This is a poetic name for the gigu vowel letter.

Identity, Tib. ngo bo: This is the name of the one sub-division of the second case. See under "case".

Immediately preceding convention, Tib. tha snyad 'das ma thags pa: A phrase used when discussing the function of the དེ་ term. It is one of several pronoun-type functions performed by this term. "Convention" refers to a spoken or written term of language which beings have agreed on to have a certain meaning.

Inclusion, Tib. sdud: There are three types of inclusion function defined in Tibetan grammar. They are carried out by a non-case linker called a separation-inclusion linker, a set of non-case linkers called ornament-inclusion linkers, and a case linker of the fifth case called a segregation-inclusion linker.

Independent linker, Tib. rang dbang gi prad: This is one of two types of phrase linker, the other being the dependent linker. See under "linker" for more.

Intertsheg, Tib. tsheg bar: The base morpheme of the English language is the word. Tibetan language has not one but two base morphemes—grammatical names and phrase linkers. The two have very different functions, but they share one morphological feature, which is that they are written with a tsheg punctuation mark on either side of them. Thus, the name for a basic unit of speech in Tibetan language is not a "word" but an "intertsheg".

Note that these have mistakenly been called "syllables" in English. This happened because they were thought to be similar to syllables of the English language. That is mistaken.

Internal divisions of cases, Tib. rnam dbye'i nang gses: Two internal divisions or sub-divisions of Tibetan cases are formally defined. See under "case" for more.

Intransitive verb, Tib. tha mi dad pa'i bya tshig: Tibetan verbs are defined as being either transitive or intransitive. The definition of transitive and intransitive is very similar to that of English grammar.

Kali, Skt. kāli: The name in Sanskrit for the consonant set. It literally means "the *string* of consonants starting with *ka*".

La-equivalent, Tib. la don: "La-equivalent" is the name given to one set of phrase linkers which collectively perform several linking functions. Unlike with some other linkers, the name "la-equivalent" does not refer to any of the functions performed but indicates that the single letter ལ་ la can perform all of the functions of the set of linkers. Thus, the other terms in the set are functionally equivalent to that letter and are given their name on that basis. There are seven la-equivalent terms.

Linker, Tib. phrad: "Linker" is the actual meaning of the Tibetan name for what Westerners have mistakenly called a "particle" till now. "Linker" is an abbreviated name; the full name is "phrase linker" (Tib. tshig phrad) *q.v.*

Linkers are of two types: dependent linkers and independent linkers. Dependent linkers change their spelling depending on the last letter of the word immediately preceding them. Because of this, each dependent linker actually consists of a group of linkers, each with a different spelling that will match one of the possible letter endings to a preceding word. Independent linkers have a constant spelling which does not change in relation to the last letter of the preceding word. Because of this, each independent linker is a single item, not a group of items with various spellings.

Name, Tib. ming: Tibetan language is built from letters. Letters are connected to each other to form one of two basic parts of speech—grammatical names and phrase linkers. A single phrase linker is then connected to a grammatical name to produce what is called a grammatical phrase. Further names and phrases are connected to form the most complex parts of speech called "expressions".

Name-base, Tib. ming gzhi: Tibetan grammatical names are built from letters. An initial consonant is set in place and it then has any of suffixes, prefixes, super-fixes, sub-fixes, and vowels added to it to make a grammatical name. The initial letter, which is the basis for the name, is thus called "the name-base".

Name's ending, Tib. ming mtha': The ending letter on a grammatical name, which will be either a suffix or re-suffix, is the name's ending. Note that, according to Thumi Saṃbhoṭa's original definition of the language, every grammatical name must have a suffix or re-suffix letter. However, in the revised form of the language that was set in place some two hundred years after that, certain cases of suffixes no longer needed to be written out. This can lead to the mis-perception that some grammatical names—for example ཉ་ nya, the word for fish—do not have a name's ending letter when in fact they do.

Naro, Tib. sna ru and na ro. This is the name of the fourth Tibetan vowel, having a sound similar to "o".

Non-case function, Tib. rnam dbye ma yin pa'i bya ba: A term used to indicate a linker that performs a function which is not a case-marking function.

Non-concordant-class segregation, Tib. mi mthun pa'i dgar ba: This is the name of one aspect of the only subdivision of the fifth or source case *q.v.* It has a matching aspect called concordant-class segregation.

Nga tsheg, Tib. nga tsheg: This is another term for the differentiating tsheg *q.v.*

Ornament and include, Tib. rgyan sdud: The type of phrase linker called an "ornament" has the two functions of ornamenting and including. See also "inclusion" for the thee types of inclusion performed by phrase linkers.

Padding, Tib. kha skong gi yi ge: See under "verse padding".

Particle: This is the name usually given by Westerners to the Tibetan part of speech called a "prad" in Tibetan. The actual meaning of the name is not "particle" but "linker". The word "particle" was in use in English grammar several centuries ago, when it was used to indicate bits of speech that did not have clearly defined functions. In Tibetan grammar, the parts of speech called "linkers" are not poorly defined bits and pieces of the Tibetan language; rather, they were regarded by Thumi Saṃbhoṭa as the most important parts of the language. Therefore, to call them "particles" is not only wrong from the point of view of the meaning of their name, but also because they are not merely bits and pieces but crucial parts of the language. See under "linker" for more.

Phrases, Tib. tshig: Tibetan language is built from letters. Letters are used to build two types of base morpheme, called grammatical names and phrase linkers. When a single phrase linker is applied to a single grammatical name, the resulting structure consisting of two intertshegs is called a "tshig". This term is often translated into English as "word". However, it is not at all like an English word. An English word is a base morpheme of the language whereas a Tibetan "tshig" is not a morpheme of the language but a more complex structure of the language that has been constructed by joining two morphemes of the language together. Moreover, it is a very specific structure, made exactly of one grammatical name and one phrase linker. It is a unique structure of the Tibetan language with no exact match in English. Therefore, because it is similar to an English phrase in that it can stand on its own but is not a complete expression, I have called it a phrase (and also a grammatical phrase in order to clearly distinguish it).

Phrase linkers, Tib. tshig phrad: Tibetan language is built from letters. Letters are connected to each other to form one of two basic parts of speech—grammatical names and phrase linkers. These parts of speech are then connected as needed to form grammatical phrases and then expressions of speech. Phrase (tshig) linkers (phrad) are, according to Thumi Saṃbhoṭa, the linchpins of Tibetan language—he says in *The Thirty* that, by understanding them properly, anyone can understand the Tibetan language.

Their name in Tibetan is exactly descriptive of their function: they are connected to grammatical names to produce grammatical phrases (Tib. tshig). These grammatical phrases are then used to make complete expressions (sentences). Thus, these parts of speech have the function of sitting in between grammatical names and other intertshegs in order to construct the language. They are exactly "phrase linkers" as their name says in Tibetan.

Phrase linkers have long been called "particles" in English publications about the Tibetan language. This is a mistake that was introduced hundreds of years ago by the first translators of Tibetan language into English and European languages. It is essential to stop calling them by an English grammar term (particle) which does not apply and to start calling them by their correct name according to Tibetan grammar—"phrase linker".

Phrase ornaments of concordance, Tib. mthun pa'i tshig rgyan: The ornament function of the class of phrase linkers called ornaments or phrase ornaments has two sub-divisions: concordant and non-concordant ornamentation.

Phrase ornaments of non-concordance, Tib. mi mthun pa'i tshig rgyan: The ornament function of the class of phrase linkers called ornaments or phrase ornaments has two sub-divisions: concordant and non-concordant ornamentation.

Prefix, Tib. sngon 'jug: The general name for a set of five letters used in name formation. These are the letters which are affixed to the front of the name-base letter. They are also called "frontings" for this reason.

Prose, Tib. tshig lhug: The name for composition not in verse.

Pure Letters, Tib. dag yig: The general name in the vocabulary of Tibetan grammar for any written work that explains the ways of the Tibetan language. It includes all types of work on grammar, dictionaries, and so on.

Recipient, Tib. 'jug yul: The particular construction of letters or the bare letter to which another letter will be connected when forming an intertsheg.

Re-suffix, Tib. yang 'jug: Two of the ten suffix letters, ད་ da and ས་ sa, can be connected to a grammatical name in the position after the suffix position. This position is then called the re-suffix position. These have incorrectly been called post-suffixes in English. A post-suffix would be any letter that follows a suffix. However, that is not the meaning here. These are the suffix letters used yet again in the suffix position. Note that the Tibetan name indicates this, literally saying "again suffix"; note that it does not use the term "post" or "after".

Re-suffix **ད་**, Tib. yang 'jug da: This is the name for the letter da when used as a re-suffix.

Re-suffix **ས་**, Tib. yang 'jug sa: This is the name for the letter sa when used as a re-suffix.

Separate and include, Tib. 'byed sdud: This is the name of a set of phrase linkers that has the two functions of separation and inclusion. See under inclusion for all types of inclusion performed by phrase linkers.

Segregation and of highlighting, Tib. dgar brnan: The phrase linker ནི་ "ni" performs two different functions called "segregation" and "highlighting".

Shad, Tib. shad: This is the name of a vertical stroke used as a punctuation mark. It has several functions. In English grammatical terms, it can function as a comma, semi-colon, and full stop.

Source, Tib. 'byung khung: This is the name of the fifth Tibetan grammatical case. Source has two sub-divisions: 1) actual source and 2) segregation and inclusion. Segregation is further divided into concordant-class and non-concordant-class segregation. See also under "case".

Source, segregate, and include: This refers to the three aspects of the fifth case: actual source case and the segregation and inclusion which are the two aspects of the sub-division of the source case. See under "source".

Speech Door Weapon, Tib. smra sgo mtshon cha: The name of a grammar text written in the eleventh century C.E. by the Indian paṇḍit Smṛitijñānakīrti who moved to Tibet and became expert in Tibetan grammar. The text is frequently quoted by later grammarians.

Suffix Tib. rjes 'jug: This is the general name for a set of ten consonant letters used in grammatical name formation. These are the letters which are affixed to the rear of the name-base letter. Two of them, the letters da and sa, can be affixed followed a suffix and are therefore called "re-suffixes".

Sub-fix, Tib. btags: There are four possible sub-fix letters when constructing a grammatical name: ya, ra, la, and wa. They are called yatag, ratag, latag, and watag or wazur respectively. See under "Grammatical name construction".

Super-fix: Tib. mgo: There are three possible super-fix letters when constructing a grammatical name: ra, la, and sa. They are called rago, lago, and sago respectively. See under "Grammatical name construction".

Ten suffixes, Tib. rjes 'jug bcu: The suffix letters are a set of ten consonants. See under suffix.

Terms of calling, Tib. bod kyi sgra: The name for the phrase linkers which have the function of hailing another person. It is the terms of the vocative case of English grammar. Terms of calling are divided into three: terms used only for hailing persons of higher social standing, terms used only for hailing persons of equal social standing, and terms used only for hailing persons of lesser social standing.

Terms of connection, Tib. 'brel ba'i sgra: The name for the phrase linkers which have the function of showing the connective case, which is the equivalent of the English genitive case.

Terms of the owner, Tib. bdag po'i sgra: The name for the group of phrase linkers which, when joined to a grammatical name, show that it refers to a person or other being. There are male, female, and generic terms of the owner. The term "owner" is a direct translation of the equivalent term in Sanskrit grammar, "pati".

Terms of generality, Tib. spyi'i sgra: The name for a set of phrase linkers which have the function of representing a general class of things or beings.

Terms of the agent, Tib. byed pa'i sgra: The name for the group of phrase linkers which represent the third case. The name is also abbreviated to "agentive terms".

Terms of the owner, Tib. bdag po'i sgra: The name for the group of phrase linkers which, when joined to a grammatical name, show that it refers to a person or other being. There are male, female, and generic terms of the owner. The term "owner" is a direct translation of the equivalent term in Sanskrit grammar, "pati".

Terms of negation, Tib. dgag pa'i sgra: The name for the group of phrase linkers which, when placed in the appropriate position, show the negation of the meaning being shown.

The Thirty, Tib. sum bcu pa: The name of the first of eight treatises on grammar by Thumi Saṃbhoṭa that defined a grammar for the Tibetan language. Its full name is *The Root of Grammar, The Thirty Verses.*

Timing, Tib. dus skabs: The name of the one sub-division of the seventh case. See under case. It is also the name of one of the five functions of the དེ་ term, in which case the Tibetan term is tshe skabs.

Transitive verb, Tib. tha dad pa'i bya tshig: Tibetan verbs are defined as being either transitive or intransitive. The definition of transitive and intransitive is very similar to that of English grammar.

Tsheg, Tib. tsheg: The name of the most frequently used of all Tibetan punctuation marks. It is a small mark with a specific shape, the size of a small dot. Its name is an onomatopoeic word equivalent to the English "snap", the sound heard when a stick, branch, or the like suddenly breaks. It is so-named because it functions literally as a break character. This fits exactly with the definition of a "break character" in typography.

Essentially speaking, it matches the use of a space in the English language to separate words. In the terminology of Tibetan grammar, it is used to separate intertshegs, *q.v.*

Verse padding, Tib. rkang skong ba'i yi ge: The name given to a letter functioning as a phrase connector which additionally is functioning to pad a line of verse so that it has the required number of intertshegs in it.

Vowel, Tib. dbyangs: The Tibetan lettering set is composed of two types of letters, no more and no less: vowels and consonants. In Tibetan language, vowels are a sound which follow the basic sound of a consonant and add a tone to it so that it is a fully-functioning letter. Therefore, the Tibetan word for vowel literally is "tone".

In Tibetan language, vowels cannot exist on their own and therefore are never written except as modifiers of a consonant. The raw sound of a vowel is obtained by starting with the ཨ་ consonant then adding the vowel to it. Vowel theory is one of the most difficult points of Tibetan grammar because the existing two of Thumi Saṃbhoṭa's eight treatises which defined Tibetan grammar do not give a complete definition of the vowels. A very extensive explanation of vowels is given in volume one of the standard references to Tibetan grammar mentioned in the introduction.

Zhabkyu, Tib. zhabs skyu: The name, literally meaning "hook down at the foot", of the second of the four Tibetan vowels, having a sound simular to "u".

About the Author, Padma Karpo Translation Committee, And Their Supports for Study

I have been encouraged over the years by all of my teachers to pass on the knowledge I have accumulated in a lifetime dedicated to study and practice, primarily in the Tibetan tradition of Buddhism. On the one hand, they have encouraged me to teach. On the other, they are concerned that, while many general books on Buddhism have been and are being published, there are few books that present the actual texts of the tradition. Therefore they, together with a number of major figures in the Buddhist book publishing world, have also encouraged me to translate and publish high quality translations of individual texts of the tradition.

My teachers always remark with great appreciation on the extraordinary amount of teaching that I have heard in this life. It allows for highly informed, accurate translations of a sort not usually seen. Briefly, I spent the 1970's studying, practising, then teaching the Gelugpa system at Chenrezig Institute, Australia, where I was a founding member and also the first Australian to be ordained as a monk in the Tibetan Buddhist tradition. In 1980, I moved to the United States to study at the feet of the Vidyādhara Chogyam Trungpa Rinpoche. I stayed in his Vajradhatu community, now called Shambhala, where I studied and practised all the Karma Kagyu, Nyingma, and Shambhala teachings being presented there and was a senior member of the Nalanda Translation Committee. After the vidyādhara's nirvana, I moved in 1992 to Nepal, where I have been continuously involved with the study, practise, translation, and teaching of the Kagyu system and especially of the Nyingma system of Great Completion. In recent years, I have spent extended times in Tibet with the greatest living Tibetan masters of Great Completion, receiving very pure transmissions of the ultimate levels of this teaching directly in Tibetan and practising them there in retreat. In that way, I have studied and practised extensively not in one Tibetan tradition as is usually done, but in three of the four Tibetan traditions—Gelug, Kagyu, and Nyingma—and also in the Theravada tradition, too.

With that as a basis, I have taken a comprehensive and long term approach to the work of translation. For any language, one first must have the lettering needed to write the language. Therefore, as a member of the Nalanda Translation Committee, I spent some years in the 1980's making Tibetan word-processing software and high-quality Tibetan fonts. After that, reliable lexical works are needed. Therefore, during the 1990's I spent some years writing the *Illuminator Tibetan-English Dictionary* and a set of treatises on Tibetan grammar, preparing a variety of key Tibetan reference works needed for the study and translation of Tibetan Buddhist texts, and giving our Tibetan software the tools needed to translate and research Tibetan texts. During this time, I also translated full-time for various Tibetan gurus and ran the Drukpa Kagyu Heritage Project—at the time the largest project in Asia for the preservation of Tibetan Buddhist texts. With the dictionaries, grammar texts, and specialized software in place, and a wealth of knowledge, I turned my attention in the year 2000 to the translation and publication of important texts of Tibetan Buddhist literature.

Padma Karpo Translation Committee (PKTC) was set up to provide a home for the translation and publication work. The committee focusses on producing books containing the best of Tibetan literature, and, especially, books that meet the needs of practitioners. At the time of writing, PKTC has published a wide range of books that, collectively, make a complete program of study for those practising Tibetan Buddhism, and especially for those interested in the higher tantras. All in all, you will find many books both free and for sale on the PKTC web-site. Most are available both as paper editions and e-books.

It would take up too much space here to present an extensive guide to our books and how they can be used as the basis for a study program. However, a guide of that sort is available on the PKTC web-site, whose address is on the copyright page of this book and we recommend that you read it to see how this book fits into the overall scheme of PKTC publications.

We have published a complete set of works on Tibetan grammar. These works are special compared to other books on the subject that have been published so far. Publications on Tibetan grammar in Western languages to date present Tibetan grammar from the perspective of Western ideas—and often incorrect ideas—about Tibetan grammar. Our publications present Tibetan grammar texts properly translated into English with extensive commentaries written on the basis of Tibetan grammar learned from the greatest Tibetan grammar experts of the author's time in classes conducted in Tibetan only and for Tibetans only.

There are two major treatises covering all the details of Tibetan grammar and with extensive explanations showing how to apply the Tibetan understanding of grammar to the Western translation of Tibetan texts. One treatise covers Thumi Saṃbhoṭa's *Thirty Verses* and the other his *Application of Gender Signs*:

- *Standard Tibetan Grammar Volume I: The Thirty Verses of Minister Thumi*, a massive treatise of several hundred pages that deals with every aspect of basic Tibetan grammar. There are long chapters on the history, revisions, and lineages of Tibetan grammar followed by authentic translations of Thumi's defining text, followed by many chapters that make clarify every aspect of the basics of Tibetan grammar. Long chapters on the cases and how they relate to English cases are included as are long chapters with thorough descriptions of every phrase linker, including ones not mentioned in *The Thirty Verses*. There are explanations of verb theory, nouns, adjectives, and other parts of speech, and punctuation.
- *Standard Tibetan Grammar Volume II: The Application of Gender Signs of Minister Thumi*, a medium-length treatise of a few hundred pages that deals with every aspect of Tibetan grammar presented in this text of Thumi. An authentic translation of Thumi's defining text is included followed by many chapters that make clarify every aspect presented in the root text. Special attention is given to the theory of transitive and intransitive verbs and how that has to be understood in order to correctly translate such Tibetan constructions into English.

Then there are a series of treatises that individually present the most common Tibetan grammar texts in use today:

- *The Great Living Tree Tibetan Grammars, Beginner's Level Tibetan Grammar Texts by Yangchen Drubpay Dorje*, the standard grammar texts currently used in all Tibetan schools as the basis for teaching Tibetan grammar together with a commentary that makes them accessible to Western readers. It is a beginner's level explanation of Thumi Saṃbhoṭa's *Thirty Verses.*
- *Tibetan Grammar: "Situ's Words", A Medium to Advanced Level Tibetan Grammar Text by Ngulchu Dharmabhadra*, the standard grammar text used to explain grammar at a medium to advanced level. It follows the system of explanation laid out in the eighth Situ Rinpoche's Great Commentary on grammar. It includes explanations of both Thumi Saṃbhoṭa's *Thirty Verses* and *Application of Gender Signs* and an extensive introduction by the author.
- *Tibetan Grammar: "The Essence of Situ's Elegant Explanation", A Medium to Advanced Level Tibetan Grammar Summarizing Situ's Great Commentary*, a grammar text that presents the eighth Situ Rinpoche's complicated and difficult to follow *Great Commentary* on grammar in an easy-to-follow presentation. It includes explanations of both Thumi Saṃbhoṭa's *Thirty Verses* and *Application of Gender Signs* and an extensive introduction by the author.
- *Tibetan Grammar: Application of Gender Signs Clarified, Advanced Tibetan Grammars by Yangchen Drubpay Dorje*, contains two important Tibetan texts that fully explain Thumi Saṃbhoṭa's defining grammar text called *Application of Gender Signs.* Thumi's text and these commentaries on it are difficult to understand, even for Tibetans, so the author has added extensive explanations which make the meaning easier to understand.

We make a point of including, where possible, the relevant Tibetan texts in Tibetan script in our books. We also make them available in electronic editions that can be downloaded free from our web-site, as discussed below. The Tibetan text for this book has not been included because of size constraints. However, a digital edition, together with the software needed to read it, is available on the PKTC web-site.

Digital Resources

PKTC has developed a complete range of software tools to facilitate the study and translation of Tibetan texts. For many years now, this software has been a prime resource for Tibetan Buddhist centres throughout the world, including in Tibet itself. It is available through the PKTC web-site.

The wordprocessor TibetDoc has the only complete set of tools for creating, correcting, and formatting Tibetan text according to the norms of the Tibetan language. It can also be used to make texts with mixed Tibetan and English or other languages. Extremely high quality Tibetan fonts, based on the forms of Tibetan calligraphy learned from old masters from pre-Communist Chinese Tibet, are also available. Because of their excellence, these typefaces have achieved a legendary status amongst Tibetans.

TibetDoc is used to prepare digital editions of Tibetan texts in the PKTC text input office in Asia. Tibetan texts are often corrupt so the input texts are carefully corrected prior to distribution. After that, they are made available through the PKTC web-site. These digital texts are not careless productions, but are highly reliable editions useful to non-scholars and scholars alike. All of these texts are available for free by immediate download.

The digital texts can be read, searched, and even made into an digital library using either TibetDoc or our other software, TibetD Reader. Like TibetDoc, TibetD Reader is advanced software with many capabilities made specifically to meet the needs of reading and researching Tibetan texts. PKTC software is for purchase but we make a free version of TibetD Reader available for download on the PKTC web-site.

A key feature of TibetDoc and Tibet Reader is that Tibetan terms in texts can be looked up on the spot using PKTC's digital dictionaries. PKTC has several digital dictionaries—some Tibetan-Tibetan and some Tibetan-English. Of them, the Illuminator Tibetan-English Dictionary is renowned for its completeness and accuracy. PKTC also offers a wide selection of important Tibetan reference works.

This combination of software, texts, dictionaries, and reference works that work together seamlessly has become famous over the years. It has been the basis of many, large publishing projects within the Tibetan Buddhist community around the world for over thirty years and is popular amongst all those needing to work with Tibetan language or deepen their understanding of Buddhism through Tibetan texts.

Tibetan Texts

༄༅། །རྟགས་ཀྱི་འཇུག་པའི་སྙིང་པོའི་དོན་མདོ་ཙམ་བརྗོད་པ་དཀའ་གནད་
གསལ་བའི་མེ་ལོང་ཞེས་བྱ་བ་བཞུགས་སོ།།

༄༅། །ན་མོ་མཉྫུ་ཤྲཱི་ཡེ། རྒྱལ་ཀུན་མཁྱེན་པའི་ཡེ་ཤེས་དབྱིངས། །གཞོན་
ནུའི་གཟུགས་ཀྱིས་རྣམ་རོལ་བ། །རྗེ་བཙུན་བརྟན་པའི་འཁོར་ལོ་དང་། །དབྱེར་
མེད་སྨྲ་བའི་ཞབས་བཏུད་ནས། །མཁས་མཆོག་ཐོན་མིའི་ཐུགས་མཆོ་ལས། །
བྱུང་བའི་བརྡ་སྤྲོད་ཕྱི་མོ་མཆོག །རྟགས་ཀྱི་འཇུག་པའི་སྙིང་པོའི་དོན། །མདོར་
བསྡུས་ཚིག་གིས་གསལ་བར་བྱ། །སྦྱོར་ནི་དབྱངས་མོ་གསལ་བྱེད་པོ། །དེ་ཕྱིར་
ཀཱ་ལི་སུམ་ཅུ་པོ། །ཕོ་ཡི་ཡི་གེ་འབའ་ཞིག་ལ། །ནང་གསེས་སྡེ་ཚན་ལྔར་དབྱེ་
སྟེ། །ཀ་ཅ་ཏ་པ་ཙ་རྣམས་ཕོ། །ཁ་ཆ་ཐ་ཕ་ཚ་མ་ནིང་། །ག་ཇ་ད་བ་ཛ་ཝ
ཞ། །ཟ་འ་ཡ་ཤ་ས་རྣམས་མོ། །ང་ཉ་ན་མ་ཤིན་ཏུ་མོ། །ར་ལ་ཧ་ཨ་མོ་གཤམ་
སྟེ། །ཨ་ནི་མཚན་མེད་ཅེས་ཀྱང་བྱ། །སྔོན་འཇུག་ལྔ་ཡི་བ་ཡིག་ཕོ། །ག་ད་
མ་ནིང་འ་མོ་ཡིག །མ་ནི་ཤིན་ཏུ་མོ་ཡིན་ནོ། །དེ་རྣམས་གང་ལ་གང་འཇུག་
ན། །ཕོ་ཡིག་བ་ནི་ཀ་ཅ་ཏ། །ཙ་ག་ང་ཛ་ཉ་ད་ན། །ཛ་ཞ་ཟ་ར་ཤ་སར་
འཇུག །མ་ནིང་ག་ནི་ཅ་ཏ་ཙ། །ཉ་ད་ན་ཞ་ཟ་ཡ་ཤ། །སར་འཇུག་མ་ནིང་ད་
ཡིག་ནི། །ཀ་པ་ག་བ་ང་མར་འཇུག །མོ་ཡིག་འ་ནི་ག་ཇ་ད། །བ་ཛ་ཁ་ཆ་ཐ

པ་ཚོར། །ཤིན་ཏུ་མོ་ཡི་མ་ཡིག་ནི། །ཁ་ཆ་ཐ་ཚ་ག་ཇ་ད། །ཛ་ང་ཉ་ན་རྣམས་
ལ་འཇུག །ཇི་ལྟར་འཇུག་པར་བྱེད་ཅེ་ན། །ཕོ་ནི་སྒྲ་རྩོལ་དྲག་པར་འཇུག །མ་
ནིང་རན་པར་འཇུག་པ་ཡིན། །མོ་ནི་ཞན་པའི་རྩོལ་གྱིས་ཏེ། །ཤིན་ཏུ་མོ་ནི་མཉམ་
པས་སོ། །ཅི་ཕྱིར་འཇུག་པར་བྱེད་ཅེ་ན། །ཐོག་མར་འདི་ལྟར་ཤེས་དགོས་
ཏེ། །ལས་གང་ཞིག་ལ་བྱེད་པ་པོ། །གཞན་དང་དངོས་སུ་འབྲེལ་བ་ཡི། །
དབང་དུ་བྱས་ནས་བྱེད་པོ་དང་། དེ་ཡི་བྱེད་པ་གཉིས་པོ་ནི། །དངོས་པོ་བདག་
ཡིན་བྱ་ཡུལ་དང་། །བྱ་བ་གཉིས་པོ་དངོས་པོ་གཞན། །དེ་བཞིན་བྱེད་པ་པོ་གཞན་
དང་། །དངོས་སུ་འབྲེལ་མིན་ཇི་ལྟར་ཡང་། །བྱ་བ་བྱས་ཟིན་འདས་པ་
དང་། །བྱ་བ་བྱེད་འགྱུར་མ་འོངས་དང་། །བྱེད་བཞིན་པ་ནི་ད་ལྟ་བ། །དེ་ཕྱིར་
དུས་གསུམ་དབྱེ་བས་ནི། །བྱེད་ལས་དང་འབྲེལ་ངག་གི་ནི། །སྦྱོར་བ་ཀུན་ལ་
ཁྱབ་པ་ཡིན། །བདག་གཞན་དབྱེ་བས་དེ་ཙམ་དུ། །ཁྱབ་པ་མིན་ཡང་བྱེད་པོ་
དང་། །བྱ་ཡུལ་བསྡུ་ཕྱིར་དབྱེ་བ་དེ། །མཛད་ནས་བདག་གཞན་དང་འབྲེལ་
བའི། །བྱ་བྱེད་རྣམས་ཀྱང་དེ་ཁོངས་བསྡུས། །དེ་ནས་དུས་གསུམ་དུ་དབྱེ་
བ། །བདག་གཞན་དབྱེ་བས་མ་ཁྱབ་པ། །བསྡུ་བའི་དོན་དུ་ཤེས་དགོས་
པར། །གསུངས་ཀྱང་སྔོན་འཇུག་འ་ཡིག་སྐབས། །བྱེད་ལས་ཙམ་དང་འབྲེལ་བ་
ཡི། །དངོས་པོ་བདག་ལའང་འཇུག་པ་མཐོང་། །དེ་ལྟར་ངེས་ནས་ཕོ་ཡིག་
ག །བསྒྲུབས་སོ་ལྟ་བུ་འདས་པ་དང་། །བསྒྲུབ་བྱའི་ལྟ་དང་བསྒྲུབ་པར་བྱ། །
ཞེས་སོགས་དངོས་པོ་གཞན་ལ་འཇུག །མ་ནིང་ག་ད་གཉིས་པོ་ནི། །གཅོད་པ་པོ་
དང་གཅོད་པར་བྱེད། །གཅོད་པར་འགྱུར་དང་དགྲི་བ་པོ། །དགྲི་བར་བྱེད་དང་
དགྲི་བར་འགྱུར། །ཞེས་སོགས་དངོས་པོ་བདག་དོན་དང་། །གཅད་བྱའི་ཤིང་
དང་གཅད་པར་བྱ། །དགྲི་བྱའི་སྣལ་མ་དགྲི་བར་བྱ། །ཞེས་སོགས་དངོས་པོ་
གཞན་དོན་དང་། །གཅོད་བཞིན་པ་དང་དགྲི་བཞིན་པ། །ཞེས་སོགས་ད་ལྟ་
བསྒྲུབ་ཆེད་འཇུག །མོ་ཡིག་འ་ནི་འཆད་པ་པོ། །འཆད་པར་བྱེད་དང་འཆད་པར་
འགྱུར། །ཞེས་སོགས་དངོས་པོ་བདག་དངོས་དང་། །འགྲོ་བ་པོ་དང་འགྲོ་བར་

བྱེད། །ཅེས་སོགས་བདག་དོན་ཕལ་པ་དང་། །འཁྲིལ་ལོ་ཞེས་སོགས་ད་ལྟ་
དང་། །འཁྲིལ་བར་འགྱུར་སོགས་མ་འོངས་འཇུག །ཤིན་ཏུ་མོ་ཡི་མ་ཡིག་
ནི། །བདག་གཞན་དུས་གསུམ་མཉམ་པར་འཇུག །འོན་ཀྱང་བྱེད་པོ་གཞན་
དངོས་དང་། །འབྲེལ་བའི་འདས་ལ་འའི་སྟོན་འཇུག །མེད་པར་ངེས་ཤིང་གད་
ཅུང་། །ད་ལྟ་བ་ལ་བའི་སྟོན་འཇུག །ཅུང་ཞིང་མགོ་ཅན་ད་ལྟ་བར། །བས་
འཕུལ་མེད་པར་ངེས་པར་ཙམ། །གཞན་ཡང་བས་འཕུལ་ཅན་ཕལ་ཆེར། །བྱེད་
པ་པོ་ནི་ད་ལྟ་དང་། །བྱ་ཡུལ་མ་འོངས་པར་བསྟུས་ནས། །འདས་ལ་བས་འཕུལ་
ཡང་འཇུག་ཡོད། །ད་ལྟ་བ་ལ་གཉིས་ཀ་མེད། །མ་འོངས་འཕུལ་ཡོད་ཡང་
འཇུག་མེད། །སྐུལ་ཚིག་འཕུལ་མེད་ཡང་འཇུག་ཡོད། །སྐབས་འགར་འདས་
དང་སྐུལ་ཚིག་ལ། །ས་རྒྱང་སྦྱར་བས་ཐུས་པའང་ཡོད། །རྗེས་འཇུག་ཡི་གེ་བཅུ་
པོ་ཡི། །ག་ད་བ་ས་བཞི་རྣམས་ཕོ། །ང་མ་འ་གསུམ་མོ་ཡིན་ཅིང་། །ན་ར་ལ་
གསུམ་མ་ནིང་སྟེ། །མིང་གཞིའི་ཡི་གེ་ཀུན་ལ་འཇུག །ཇི་ལྟར་འཇུག་ཚུལ་
གཉིས་ཡིན་ཏེ། །དང་པོ་སྦྲ་ཡི་འཇུག་ཚུལ་ནི། །ཕོ་ཡི་ག་ཡིག་ཡང་འཇུག་
ཅན། །སྐྱེས་བུ་རབ་དང་ཕོ་ཡིག་བ། །ཡང་འཇུག་ཅན་ནི་སྐྱེས་བུ་འབྲིང་། །
ག་བ་ཡང་འཇུག་མེད་པ་དང་། །ད་སའི་མཐའ་ཅན་ཐ་མ་སྟེ། །དྲག་པ་ཕོ་ལའང་
ནང་གསེས་ཀྱིས། །དྲག་ཞན་བར་མ་གསུམ་དུ་དབྱེ། །དེ་བཞིན་ཞན་པ་མོ་ལ་
ཡང་། །ནང་གསེས་དྲག་ཞན་གཉིས་དབྱེ་སྟེ། །ང་མ་ཡང་འཇུག་ཅན་མོ་
དང་། །ང་མ་ཡང་འཇུག་མེད་པ་དང་། །འ་མཐའ་ཅན་རྣམས་ཤིན་ཏུ་མོ། །
བར་མ་མ་ནིང་ན་ར་ལ། །ཡང་འཇུག་ཡོད་དམ་མེད་ཀྱང་རུང་། །མིང་གཞི་ཕོ་
ཡིག་མཐར་ཡོད་དང་། །མིང་གཞི་མ་ནིང་རྗེས་སུ་ནི། །ཡང་འཇུག་དང་བཅས་
ཞུགས་པ་ན། །དྲག་དང་འཕྲད་པས་དྲག་པར་འགྱུར། །མིང་གཞི་མོ་ཡིག་རྗེས་
སུ་ནི། །ཡང་འཇུག་མེད་པར་ཞུགས་པ་ན། །ཞན་དང་འཕྲད་པས་ཞན་པར་
འགྱུར། །དེ་གཉིས་འགྱུར་བ་མ་ནིང་ཡིན། །མིང་གཞི་མོ་ཡིག་རྗེས་སུ་ནི། །
ཡང་འཇུག་དང་བཅས་ཞུགས་པ་ན། །དྲག་ཞན་གཉིས་ཀའི་ཆ་ལྡན་ཕྱིར། །

མཚན་གཉིས་མ་ནིང་ཞེས་སུ་གྲགས། །མིང་གཞི་མ་ནིང་རྗེས་སུ་ནི། །ཡང་
འཇུག་མེད་པར་ཞུགས་པ་ན། །དྲག་ཞན་གང་དུའང་མི་འགྱུར་བས། །མཚན་
མེད་མ་ནིང་ཞེས་སུ་འདོད། །གཉིས་པ་དོན་ལ་གཉིས་ཡོད་པའི། །སྔ་མ་གང་
ལྟར་འགྱུར་བ་ནི། །རྗེས་འཇུག་གང་ལ་བཞུགས་པ་ཡི། །མིང་དེས་བདག་
གཞན་སོགས་གང་སྟོན། །ཕལ་ཆེར་མིང་དེའི་སྟོན་འཇུག་གི །ནུས་པར་སྦྱར་
ནས་རྟོགས་པར་བྱ། །ཕྱི་མ་ཇི་ལྟར་འགྱུར་བ་ནི། །རྗེས་འཇུག་ཕོ་ཡིས་ཕོ་ཡིག་གི
།མིང་མཐའ་གཞན་དྲངས་དེ་བཞིན་དུ། །མོ་ཡིས་མོ་ཡི་མིང་མཐའ་དང་། །མ་
ནིང་གིས་ནི་མ་ནིང་དྲངས། །དེ་རྣམས་རྟགས་མཚུངས་འདྲེན་ཚུལ་ཏེ། །བརྗོད་
བདེ་འདྲེན་པའང་ཤིན་ཏུ་མང་། །གཞན་ཡང་མིང་མཐའ་དེ་ཉིད་ཀྱིས། །རྟགས་
མཚུངས་པ་འམ་སྒྲ་མཐུན་པའི། །རྣམ་དབྱེ་བརྒྱད་དང་སླར་བསྡུ་སོགས། །སྔ་
མའི་ཤུགས་དང་མཐུན་པར་འདྲེན། །དེ་དག་ནང་གསེས་གང་འཇུག་ནི། །རྣམ་
དབྱེའམ་འཕྲད་ཅེས་མིང་ཚིག་དེའི། །མཐའ་སྦྱར་མིང་དོན་ལས་ཤེས་བྱ། །དེ་
ཡང་ཆོས་རྣམས་ངོ་བོ་ཙམ། །བརྗོད་པ་རྣམ་དབྱེ་དང་པོ་སྟེ། །དཔེར་ན་བུམ་པ་ཀ་
བ་བཞིན། །གསལ་བྱེད་བོད་ཀྱི་སྐད་ལ་ཉུང་། །ལས་དང་བྱ་ཡུལ་དོན་གཅིག་
སྟེ། །དེ་ལྟའི་བྱ་བའི་ཡུལ་ཞིག་ལ། །བྱ་བ་བྱས་པར་སྟོན་པ་ལ། །གཉིས་པ་
ལས་སུ་བྱ་བ་དང་། །གཉིས་པའི་ནང་ཚན་དེ་ཉིད་དང་། །བཞི་པ་དགོས་ཆེད་
གསུམ་འདྲ་ཡང་། །བྱ་བ་བྱས་པས་བྱ་བའི་ཡུལ། །དེ་འམ་དེ་དང་འབྲེལ་བ་
ལ། །ཕན་ཐོགས་མེད་ན་གཉིས་པ་སྟེ། །དཔེར་ན་ཤར་དུ་འགྲོ་ལྟ་བུ། །ཕན་
ཐོགས་ཡོད་ན་བཞི་པ་སྟེ། །དཔེར་ན་སློང་ལ་སྦྱིན་ལྟ་བུ། །ཕན་ཐོགས་མེད་ཀྱང་
བྱ་ཡུལ་དང་། །བྱ་བ་ངོ་བོ་གཅིག་ཡིན་ན། །གཉིས་པའི་ནང་ཚན་དེ་ཉིད་དེ། །
དཔེར་ན་ལྷ་རུ་གསལ་ལྟ་བུ། །གང་ཞིག་གང་ལ་བརྟེན་པའམ། །གནས་དང་
ཡོད་པའི་དོན་ཙམ་ལས། །བྱ་བ་གཏན་ནས་མི་བྱེད་ན། །རྣམ་དབྱེ་བདུན་པ་
གནས་གཞི་སྟེ། །དཔེར་ན་སྟེང་དུ་མི་ཡོད་ལྟར། །ཚེ་སྐབས་གཉིས་དང་དོན་འདྲ་
ན། །བདུན་པའི་ནང་ཚན་ཚེ་སྐབས་ཏེ། །དཔེར་ན་མཚུ་ཟླ་ཤར་བ་ན། །ཚེ་

འཕྲུལ་དུས་ཆེན་ཚུགས་ལྟ་བུ། །རྣམ་དབྱེ་གཉིས་བཞི་བདུན་པ་དང་། །དེ་ཉིད་ཚེ་
སྐབས་གསལ་བྱེད་སྒྲ། །སུ་ར་རུ་དུ་ན་ལ་ཏུ། །ཡིན་ཞིང་ཕལ་ཆེར་ལ་སྒྲ་
དང་། །མཐུན་པས་ལ་དོན་རྣམ་དབྱེའང་ཟེར། །འོན་ཀྱང་ན་ལ་དེ་ཉིད་ལ། །
མི་འཇུག་སླ་བའི་སྒོ་ལས་གསུངས། །རྣམ་དབྱེ་གང་ལ་སྦྱོར་ཡུལ་དེས། །ཉེ་
འགྱུར་གང་དུ་བྱ་བ་ཞིག །བྱས་ན་གསུམ་པ་བྱེད་སྒྲ་སྟེ། །དཔེར་ན་བདག་གིས་
བཤད་ལྟ་བུ། །བྱ་བ་གཏན་ནས་མི་བྱེད་པར། །སྤྱི་ཡི་འབྲེལ་བྱེད་ཙམ་སྟོན་
ན། །རྣམ་དབྱེ་དྲུག་པ་འབྲེལ་སྒྲ་སྟེ། །དཔེར་ན་བདག་གི་མིག་ལྟ་བུ། །རྣམ་
དབྱེ་གསུམ་དྲུག་གསལ་བྱེད་སྒྲ། །ས་མཐའ་ཡོད་དང་མེད་པ་ཡི། །གི་ཀྱི་གྱི་འི་
ཡི་ལྟ་ཡིན། །གང་ཞིག་གང་ལས་བྱུང་བའམ། །བྱེ་དང་ལྷུང་བའི་དོན་ལྡན་
ན། །རྣམ་དབྱེ་ལྔ་པ་འབྱུང་ཁུངས་ཏེ། །དཔེར་ན་ཞལ་ནས་ཐོས་ལྟ་བུ། །
གསལ་བྱེད་སྒྲ་ནི་ནས་ལས་ཏེ། །དགར་དང་སྡུད་པའང་ལྔ་པར་གཏོགས། །
གཞན་ཡང་ཚིག་དོན་གོང་འོག་ཏུ། །བསྡུ་རྒྱུ་ཡོད་ན་སྡུད་པའི་སྒྲ། །དང་དང་
ཀྱང་ཡང་འང་སོགས་སྦྱོར། །རྣམ་གྲངས་དུ་མས་དོན་བསྐྱར་ན། །འབྱེད་སྡུད་སྒྲ་
འཇུག་དགག་པ་དང་། །བདག་དོན་ཡོད་ན་ཐོག་མཐའ་རུ། །པ་སྟེའི་རྟགས་
རྣམས་ཅི་རིགས་འཇུག །རྒྱུན་དུ་གྱུར་པའི་ཚིག་ཕྲད་ཀྱང་། །དོན་ལ་བསླེགས་ས་
ཡོད་ན་སྦྱོར། །དེ་བཞིན་བསྟན་བྱ་ལྷག་ཡོད་ན། །ལྷག་བཅས་སྒྲ་སྦྱོར་ཚིག་དོན་
ནི། །རྫོགས་ན་སླར་སྡུའི་སྒྲ་རྣམས་སྦྱོར། །དགོས་པ་ཅི་ཕྱིར་འཇུག་ཅེ་ན། །
མོ་ཡིག་དབྱངས་དང་མི་ལྡན་ན། །ཕོ་ཡིག་གསལ་བྱེད་བརྗོད་མི་ནུས། །དེ་ཕྱིར་
དབྱངས་ལྡར་བཞེད་པ་བདེ། །ཕོ་ཡིག་དབྱངས་ལྡན་དེ་དག་ལའང་། །རྗེས་
འཇུག་བཅུ་པོ་མ་ཞུགས་ན། །དོན་གྱི་ངོ་བོ་ཙམ་སྟོན་པའི། །མིང་དང་དོན་གྱི་ཁྱད་
པར་རྣམས། །སྟོན་པའི་ཚིག་དང་དོན་ལྡན་པའི། །ངག་གི་བརྗོད་པ་ཡོད་མིན་
ཏེ། །ཡི་གེའི་ཁོངས་ནས་མིང་དབྱུང་ཞིང་། མིང་གི་ཁོངས་ནས་ཚིག་ཕྱུངས་
ནས། །ཚིག་གིས་དོན་རྣམས་སྟོན་པས་སོ། །མིང་ཚིག་བརྗོད་པ་མེད་ན་ནི། །
མཐུན་མོང་མཐུན་མོང་མ་ཡིན་པའི། །ཤེས་བྱ་སྟོན་པའང་མེད་པར་འགྱུར། །དེ་

ཕྱིར་འཕགས་ཡུལ་མཁས་རྣམས་ཀྱི། །རྗེས་སུ་འབྲངས་ནས་གསུངས་པ་
འདི། །སྐྱེ་བོ་ཀུན་གྱིས་རྟོགས་ཕྱུར་ཅིག །ཚིག་གི་སྦྲ་ཙམ་འདྲ་ན་ཡང་། །
དོན་ལ་ཁྱད་པར་ཤིན་ཏུ་ཆེ། །དེ་ཕྱིར་བརྡ་དག་ལ་བརྟེན་ནས། །མ་ནོར་དོན་
རྣམས་འཚོལ་བ་གཅེས། །དོན་ལ་མི་རྨོངས་རྨོངས་པ་ཡང་། །ལུགས་འདིར་
མཁས་མིན་གྱིས་བྱེད་དེ། །སྒྲ་ཤེས་དོན་ལ་མི་རྨོངས་ཞེས། །མཁས་པའི་གསུང་
ལ་ཡོངས་སུ་གྲགས། །འདི་ལ་མ་སྦྱངས་རྨོངས་ཚོད་ཀྱིས། །འཆད་རྩོད་རྩོམ་
པའི་གྲྭར་འཇུག་པ། །ཞ་སྐྱེས་སེང་ལྤགས་གྱོན་པ་བཞིན། །ནམ་ཞིག་རྗེས་ངན་
གསལ་བར་འགྱུར། །དེ་ཕྱིར་བློ་གསལ་དོན་གཉེར་རྣམས། །རྟགས་འཇུག་
དཀའ་གནད་གཟུགས་བརྙན་ཀུན། །གསལ་བར་འཆར་བའི་མེ་ལོང་འདིར། །
ལ་འུར་གཟིགས་མོར་སྤྱོན་དང་ཀྱེ། །འདི་ལ་ནོངས་པའི་ཚོགས་མཆིས་ན། །
གཟུར་གནས་མཁས་པའི་སྤྱན་སྔར་འཆགས། །ཅུང་ཟད་འབད་ལས་ཐོབ་པའི་
དགེས། །ཀུན་གྱིས་འདི་དོན་རྟོགས་པར་ཤོག །ཅེས་རྟགས་ཀྱི་འཇུག་པའི་སྙིང་
པོའི་དོན་མདོ་ཙམ་བརྗོད་པ་དཀའ་གནད་གསལ་བའི་མེ་ལོང་ཞེས་བྱ་བ་འདི་ནི།
རང་གི་སློབ་བུ་རྗེ་དྲུང་སངས་རྒྱས་རྒྱ་མཚོ་དང་དོན་གྲུབ་ཕུན་ཚོགས་གཉིས་ནས་དགོས་
ཚུལ་ལྟར། མཁས་མཆོག་སི་ཏུ་པཎ་ཆེན་དང་ཐམས་ཅད་མཁྱེན་པ་ཛྙཱ་བྷ་དྲ་དཔལ་
བཟང་པོའི་བཞེད་པ་དང་མཐུན་པར་དབྱངས་ཅན་གྲུབ་པའི་རྡོ་རྗེས་སྦྱར་བའོ།།
||

༄༅། །རྟགས་འཇུག་དཀའ་གནད་གསལ་བའི་མེ་ལོང་གི་འགྲེལ་པ་རིག་ལམ་གསེར་གྱི་ལྡེ་མིག་ཅེས་བྱ་བ་བཞུགས་སོ།།

༄༅། །ན་མོ་མཉྫུ་ཤྲཱི་ཡེ། མཁའ་ཁྱབ་ཤེས་བྱ་ཡོངས་ཀྱི་གཤིས་ལུགས་ཆོས། །བརྗོད་བྲལ་འགྱུར་མེད་དབྱིངས་སུ་མངོན་གཟིགས་པ། །རྒྱལ་བ་ཀུན་ལས་བཀའ་དྲིན་ལྷག་པའི་མགོན། །དཀའ་འགྱུར་ཆོས་ཀྱི་རྒྱལ་པོ་གཙུག་ན་རྒྱལ། །དུས་གསུམ་རྒྱལ་བའི་ཡེ་ཤེས་མ་ལུས་པ། །གཅིག་བསྡུས་རང་གཟུགས་སྨྲ་བ་ངག་གི་ལྷ། །བརྒྱད་གཉིས་ལང་ཚོའི་འཛུམ་སྒེག་གར་རྩེན་པ། །འཇམ་དཔལ་རྡོ་རྗེ་རྣོན་པོས་དགེ་ལེགས་སྩོལ། །བརྒྱད་ཁྲི་བཞི་སྟོང་ཆོས་ཚུལ་ཏམ་བུ་རའི། །སྒྲ་ལས་དྲངས་པའི་དབྱངས་ཀྱི་དཀྱིལ་འཁོར་ཀུན། །སྐལ་བཟང་བློས་འཛིན་དཔྱིད་དུ་འཛོམ་མཛད་མ། །སྒྲ་ལྡན་ལྷ་མོ་སྙིང་ལ་རོལ་བར་མཛོད། །དབྱངས་ཅན་ཐུགས་ལ་གྲུབ་པའི་རྡོ་རྗེ་ཡི། །ཟབ་ཡངས་བློ་གྲོས་མཐོ་རིས་སྐྱེད་ཚལ་ལས། །ལེགས་འོངས་རྟགས་འཇུག་པད་མ་འཛུམ་པའི་ཞལ། །རྣམ་དཔྱོད་ཉིན་བྱེད་སྣང་བས་དབྱེ་བར་བྱ། །ཀུ་ཡེ་བློ་གསལ་ཁྱང་དྲུག་གཞོན་ནུ་རྣམས། །བརྡ་དག་སྦྲང་རྩིའི་དགའ་སྟོན་སྤྱོད་འདོད་ན། །ལེགས་བཤད་མེ་ཏོག་ཁ་སྒོ་ཕྱེ་བའི་དུས། །དགའ་བའི་གླུ་དབྱངས་དང་བཅས་ཞུགས་པར་རིགས། །དེ་ལ་འདིར་སྐབས་དུས་ཀྱི་པཎྜི་ཏ་ཆེན་པོ་དངུལ་ཆུ་དབྱངས་ཅན་གྲུབ་པའི་རྡོ་རྗེ་དཔལ་བཟང་པོས་མཛད་པའི་ལེགས་བཤད་རྨད་དུ་བྱུང་བ་རྟགས་འཇུག་དཀའ་གནད་གསལ་བའི་མེ་ལོང་འདི་ཉིད་ས་བཅད་རྒྱས་པ་སོགས་དོར་ནས་མདོར་བསྡུས་སུ་འཆད་པ་ལ་གསུམ། མཆོད་བརྗོད། བརྩམ་པར་དམ་བཅའ། གཞུང་དོན་དངོས་སོ། །དང་པོ་མཆོད་བརྗོད་ལ་ཡང་རྒྱ་སྐད་དང་བོད་སྐད་གཉིས་ལས་དང་པོ་རྒྱ་སྐད་ཀྱི་སྒོ་ནས་མཆོད་བརྗོད་ནི། ན་མོ་མཉྫུ་ཤྲཱི་ཡེ། །ཞེས་པ། །བྱང་ཕྱོགས་ཁ་བ་ཅན་པ་སྟོད་མངའ་རིས་སྐོར་གསུམ་རྫིང་བུ་ལྟ་བུ། བར་དབུས་གཙང་རུ་བཞི་ཡུར་བ་ལྟ་བུ། སྨད་མདོ་ཁམས་སྒང་དྲུག་ཞིང་ས་དང་འདྲ་བར་ཡོད་ལ། དེ་ལ་ཡང་བོད་དང་བོད་ཆེན་

པོ་གཉིས་ལས་བོད་དབུས་གཙང་གི་སྐད་དུ། ན་མོ་ཕྱག་འཚལ་ལོ། །མཉྫུ་འཇམ། ཤྲཱི་དཔལ། ཡེ་ལ་སྨྲ། འཇམ་དཔལ་ལ་ཕྱག་འཚལ་ལོ། །ཞེས་པའོ། །གཉིས་པ་བོད་སྐད་ཀྱི་སྒོ་ནས་མཆོད་པར་བརྗོད་པ་ནི། རྒྱལ་ཀུན་མཁྱེན་པའི་ཡེ་ཤེས་དབྱིངས། །གཞོན་ནུའི་གཟུགས་ཀྱིས་རྣམ་རོལ་པ། །རྗེ་བཙུན་བརྟན་པའི་འཁོར་ལོ་དང་། །དབྱེར་མེད་བླ་མའི་ཞབས་བཏུད་ནས། །ཞེས་པ། རབ་འབྱམས་རྒྱལ་བ་ཀུན་གྱི་མཁྱེན་རབ་ཀྱི་ཡེ་ཤེས་གཅིག་ཏུ་བསྡུས་པའི་དབྱིངས་དེ་སྙིང་པོ། །གཞོན་ནུ་ན་ཚོད་བཅུ་དྲུག་ལོན་པའི་གཟུགས་ཀྱིས་རྣམ་པར་རོལ་པ། རྗེ་བཙུན་བརྟན་པའི་འཁོར་ལོ་སྟེ་འཇམ་དཔལ་དབྱངས་དང་ངོ་བོ་དབྱེར་མེད་པའི་རང་ལ་མངོན་མཐོ་དང་ངེས་ལེགས་ཀྱི་ལམ་མ་ནོར་བར་སྟོན་པའི་ཐམས་ཅད་མཁྱེན་པ་རྟྣ་བྷ་དྲ་སོགས་དངོས་བརྒྱུད་བླ་མ་རྣམས་ཀྱི་ཞབས་ཀྱི་པད་མོ་ལ་སྒོ་གསུམ་གུས་པ་ཆེན་པོས་བཏུད་ནས། །ཞེས་པའོ། །གཉིས་པ་བརྩམ་པར་དམ་བཅའ་ནི། །མཁས་མཆོག་ཐོན་མིའི་ཐུགས་མཚོ་ལས། །འབྱུང་བའི་བརྡ་སྤྲོད་ཕྱི་མོ་མཆོག །རྟགས་ཀྱི་འཇུག་པའི་སྙིང་པོའི་དོན། །མདོར་བསྡུས་ཚིག་གིས་གསལ་བར་བྱ། །ཞེས་པ། གངས་ཅན་སྣ་ལའི་སྨན་ལྗོངས་འདིར་མཁས་གྲུབ་ནམ་མཁའི་སྐར་ཚོགས་ལྟར་བྱོན་པ་རྣམས་ཀྱི་ནང་ནས་མཆོག་ཏུ་གྱུར་པ་ཐོན་མི་ཉིད་ཀྱི་ཐུགས་ཀྱི་རྒྱ་མཚོ་ཆེན་པོ་ལས་བྱུང་བའི་ཡུལ་གངས་ཅན་གྱི་སྐད་ཀྱི་བརྡ་སྤྲོད་པའི་བསྟན་བཅོས་ཀུན་གྱི་ཕྱི་མོ་ལམ་མ་ཕྱི་ལམ་གཞི་ལམ་རྩ་བ་མཆོག་ཏུ་གྱུར་པ་སུམ་རྟགས་གཉིས་ལས་རྟགས་ཀྱི་འཇུག་པའི་སྙིང་པོའི་དོན་རྣམས་མ་ཚང་བ་མེད་པར་མདོར་བསྡུས་པའི་ཚིག་སྒོ་ནས་གསལ་བར་བྱ། །ཞེས་པའོ། །གསུམ་པ་གཞུང་དོན་དངོས་ནི། །སྤྱིར་ན་དབྱངས་མོ་གསལ་བྱེད་ཕོ། །དེ་ཕྱིར་ཀཱ་ལི་སུམ་ཅུ་པོ། །ཞེས་པ། །མིང་གཞིའི་ཡི་གེ་སྤྱིའི་རྟགས་ཀྱི་དབྱེ་བ་བཤད་པ་སྟེ། སྤྱིར་ཡི་གེ་ལ་དབྱེ་ན་དབྱངས་དང་གསལ་བྱེད་གཉིས་སུ་ཡོད། དེ་ལས་དབྱངས་ཀྱི་བྱ་བ་གསལ་བར་མཚོན་པར་བྱེད་པ། ཨི་སྟེ་གི་གུ། ཨུ་སྟེ་ཞབས་ཀྱུ། ཨེ་སྟེ་འགྲེང་བུ། ཨོ་སྟེ་ན་རོ་བཞི་ནི་མོ་དང་། ཀཱ་ལིའི་བྱ་བ་གསལ་བར་བྱེད་པའི་ཀ་ནས་ཨའི་བར་གྱི་ཡི་གེ་སུམ་ཅུ་

པོ་རྣམས་ནི་ཕོར་ཤེས་པར་བྱའོ། །ཞེས་པའོ། །ཕོ་ཡི་ཡི་གེ་འབའ་ཞིག་ལ། །ནང་གསེས་སྡེ་ཚན་ལྔར་དབྱེ་སྟེ། །ཞེས་པ། ཕོ་ཡིག་སུམ་ཅུ་པོ་དེ་རྣམས་ནང་གསེས་སྡེ་ཚན་སོ་སོར་དབྱེ་ན་ལྔར་འགྱུར་ཏེ། ལྔ་གང་ཞེ་ན། ཕོ་དང་། མ་ནིང་དང་། མོ་དང་། ཤིན་ཏུ་མོ་དང་། མོ་གཤམ་སྟེ་ལྔར་འགྱུར་རོ། །འབའ་ཞིག་ནི་ཁོ་ན་ཞེས་པའི་དོན་ནོ། །དེ་ལྔའི་དང་པོ་ཕོ་ནི། ཀ་ཅ་ཏ་པ་ཙ་རྣམས་ཕོ། །ཞེས་པ། ཀ་དང་། ཅ་དང་། ཏ་དང་། པ་དང་། ཙ་བཅས་ལྔ་པོ་དེ་རྣམས་ཕོ་ཡིག་གོ །གཉིས་པ་མ་ནིང་ནི། ཁ་ཆ་ཐ་ཕ་ཚ་མ་ནིང་། །ཞེས་པ། ཁ་དང་། ཆ་དང་། ཐ་དང་། ཕ་དང་། ཚ་བཅས་ལྔ་ནི་མ་ནིང་གི་ཡི་གེའོ། །གསུམ་པ་མོ་ནི། ག་ཇ་ད་བ་ཛ་ཝ་ཞ་ཟ་འ་ཡ་ཤ་ས་རྣམས་མོ། །ཞེས་པ། ག་དང་། ཇ་དང་། ད་དང་། བ་དང་། ཛ་དང་། ཝ་དང་། ཞ་དང་། ཟ་དང་། འ་དང་། ཡ་དང་། ཤ་དང་། ས་བཅས་བཅུ་གཉིས་པོ་འདི་རྣམས་མོ་ཡིག་གོ །བཞི་པ་ཤིན་ཏུ་མོ་ནི། ང་ཉ་ན་མ་ཤིན་ཏུ་མོ། །ཞེས་པ། ང་དང་། ཉ་དང་། ན་དང་། མ་བཅས་བཞི་པོ་ཤིན་ཏུ་མོའི་ཡི་གེའོ། །ལྔ་པ་མོ་གཤམ་གྱི་ཡི་གེ་ནི། ར་ལ་ཧ་ཨ་མོ་གཤམ་སྟེ། །ཞེས་པ། ར་དང་། ལ་དང་། ཧ་དང་། ཨ་དང་བཅས་བཞི་ནི་མོ་གཤམ་གྱི་ཡི་གེའོ། །ཨ་ནི་མཚན་མེད་ཅེས་ཀྱང་བྱ། །ཞེས་པ། ཨ་ནི་མོ་གཤམ་གྱི་ཡི་གེ་ཡིན་པར་མ་ཟད། སྒྲ་རྩོལ་ཤིན་ཏུ་ཞན་པས་མཚན་མེད་ཅེས་ཀྱང་བྱ་བ་སྟེ་ཟེར་བ་ཡིན་ནོ། ཞེས་པའོ། །སྔོན་འཇུག་ལྔ་ཡི་བ་ཡིག་ཕོ། །ཞེས་པ། སྔོན་འཇུག་གི་རྟགས་ཀྱི་དབྱེ་བ་བཤད་པ་སྟེ། རང་གི་འཇུག་ཡུལ་དུ་གྱུར་བའི་མིང་གཞིའི་སྔོན་དུ་འཇུག་པའི་སྔོན་འཇུག་ལྔ་ནི། ལེགས་བཤད་ལྗོན་དབང་ལས། །གད་བམ་འ་སྔོན་འཇུག །ཅེས་པ་ལྟར་སྔོན་འཇུག་ལྔ་པོ་དེའི་ནང་ནས་བ་ཡིག་ནི་ཕོ་ཡིན་ནོ། །ག་ད་མ་ནིང་འ་མོ་ཡིག །ཅེས་པ། ག་ད་གཉིས་སྔོན་འཇུག་གི་མ་ནིང་དང་། །འོ་མ་ཡིག་ཅེས་པ་འ་ནི་མོ་དང་། མ་ནི་ཤིན་ཏུ་མོར་འགྱུར་བ་ཡིན་ནོ། །དེ་རྣམས་གང་ལ་གང་འཇུག་ན། །ཞེས་པ། སྔོན་འཇུག་གི་རྟགས་ཀྱི་

འཇུག་པ་བཤད་པ་སྟེ། གོང་དུ་བཤད་པའི་ཡི་གེ་དེ་རྣམས་མིང་གཞིའི་ཡི་གེ་གང་ལ་
སྔོན་འཇུག་གང་འཇུག་ཅེ་ན། །ཕོ་ཡིག་བ་ནི་ཀ་ཅ་ཏ། །ཙ་ག་ང་ཇ་ཉ་ད་ན། །
ཛ་ཞ་ཟ་ར་ཤ་སར་འཇུག །ཅེས་པ། སྔོན་འཇུག་གི་ཕོ་ཡིག་བ་ནི། ཀ་དང་།
ཅ་དང་། ཏ་དང་། ཙ་དང་། ག་དང་། ང་དང་། ཇ་དང་། ཉ་དང་།
ད་དང་། ན་དང་། ཛ་དང་། ཞ་དང་། ཟ་དང་། ར་དང་། ཤ་དང་།
ས་བཅས་ཡི་གེ་བཅུ་དྲུག་པོ་འདི་རྣམས་ལ་འཇུག་ཅིང་ཀ་ལ་རྐྱང་བརྩེགས་འདོགས་
གསུམ་གྱི་སྒོ་ནས་འཇུག་པ་ནི། དཔེར་ན། བཀའ། བསྐ། བཀྱེ།
བཀྲ། བསྐྱངས། ཅ་ལ་རྐྱང་འཕུལ་ཕོ་ནས་འཇུག་པ་དཔེར་ན། བཅས།
བཅོམ། བཅུག ལྟ་བུ། ཏ་ལ་རྐྱང་བརྩེགས་གཉིས་ཀྱིས་འཇུག་སྟེ་དཔེར་ན།
བཏབ། བཏུད། བཏགས། བརྟགས། བལྟ། བསྟར། ལྟ་བུ།
ཙ་ལ་རྐྱང་བརྩེགས་ཀྱིས་འཇུག་པ་ནི། བཙལ། བཙོས། བརྩུགས།
བརྩེགས། ལྟ་བུ། ག་ལ་རྐྱང་འདོགས་བརྩེགས་གསུམ་གྱིས་འཇུག་པ་ནི།
བགོ། བགྲང་། བགྱིས། བརྒྱལ། བསྒོམས། ལྟ་བུ། ང་ལ་
བརྩེགས་འཕུལ་ཕོ་ནས་འཇུག་པ་ནི། བརྔམས། བསྔགས། ལྟ་བུ། ཇ་
ལ་བརྩེགས་འཕུལ་ཕོ་ནས་འཇུག་པ། བརྗེས། བརྗིད། ལྟ་བུ། ཉ་ལ་
བརྩེགས་འཕུལ་ཕོ་ནས། བརྙན། བསྙེན། ལྟ་བུ། ད་ལ་རྐྱང་བརྩེགས་
གཉིས་ཀྱིས་འཇུག་པ་ནི། བདེ། བརྡ། བལྡུག །བསྡད། ལྟ་བུ།
ན་ལ་བརྩེགས་འཕུལ་ཕོ་ནས། བརྣག བསྣམས། ལྟ་བུ། ཛ་ལ་བརྩེགས་
འཕུལ་ཕོ་ནས་འཇུག་པ་ནི། བརྫེས། བརྫིས། ལྟ་བུ། ཞ་ལ་རྐྱང་འཕུལ།
བཞག བཞི། བཞེས། ལྟ་བུ། ཟ་ལ་རྐྱང་འདོགས་གཉིས། དཔེར་ན།
བཟང་། བཟི། བཟུང་། བཟེད། བཟློ། བཟླས། ལྟ་བུ། ར་ལ་
འདོགས་འཕུལ་ཕོ་ནས་འཇུག་པ་ནི། བརླབས། ལྟ་བུ། ཤ་ལ་རྐྱང་འཕུལ་ཕོ་
ནས་འཇུག་པ་ནི། དཔེར་ན། བཤད། བཤེས། ལྟ་བུ། ས་ལ་རྐྱང་
འདོགས་གཉིས་ཀྱིས་འཇུག་པ། བསམ། བསུ། བསེ། བསོས།

བསྲིས། བསྲུངས། བསྲེས། བསྲོས། བསླབ། ལྟ་བུ། མ་ཉིང་
ག་ཉི་ཅ་ཏ་ཙོ། །ཉ་ད་ན་ཞ་ཟ་ཡ་ཤ། །སར་འཇུག །ཅེས་པ། སྔོན་འཇུག
གི་མ་ཉིང་ག་ཉི་མིང་གཞིའི། ཅ་དང་། ཏ་དང་། ཙོ་དང་། ཉ་དང་། ད་
དང་། ན་དང་། ཞ་དང་། ཟ་དང་། ཡ་དང་། ཤ་དང་། ས་བཅས་
བཅུ་གཅིག་ལ་རྐྱང་འཕུལ་ཁོ་ནས་འཇུག་པ་ནི། གཅོད། གཏེར། གཙོ།
གཉེན། གདོང་། གནད། གཞལ། གཟིགས། གཡང་།
གཤེགས། གསུང་། ལྟ་བུ། མ་ཉིང་ད་ཡིག་ནི། ཀ་པ་ག་བ་ང་མར་
འཇུག །ཅེས་པ། སྔོན་འཇུག་གི་མ་ཉིང་ད་ཡིག་ནི་མིང་གཞིའི། ཀ་དང་།
པ་དང་། ག་དང་། བ་དང་། ང་དང་། མ་བཅས་དྲུག་པོ་འདི་རྣམས་ལ་
འཇུག་ཅིང་། དེ་ཡང་ང་ལ་རྐྱང་འཕུལ་དང་གཞན་ལྔ་ལ་རྐྱང་འདོགས་གཉིས་ཏེ།
དཔེར་ན། དཀར། དཀྱིལ། དཀྲིགས། དཔལ། དཔྲལ། དཔྱིད།
དགའ། དགྲ། དགྱེས། དབང་། དབྲི། དབྱིབས། དངུལ།
དམའ། དམིགས། དམྱལ། ལྟ་བུ། མོ་ཡིག་འ་ནི་ག་ཇ་ད། །བ་ཛོ་ཁ་
ཆ་ཐ་ཕ་ཚོར། །ཞེས་པ། ག་དང་། ཇ་དང་། ད་དང་། བ་དང་། ཛོ་
དང་། ཁ་དང་། ཆ་དང་། ཐ་དང་། ཕ་དང་། ཚོ་དང་། བཅས་
བཅུ་པོ་ལ་མོ་ཡིག་འ་འཇུག་པ་ལས། ག་ལ་རྐྱང་འདོགས་གཉིས་ཀྱི་འཇུག་པ་ནི།
འགའ། འགྲོ། འགྱེལ། ཇ་ལ་རྐྱང་འཕུལ་ནི། འཇལ། ད་ལ་རྐྱང་
འདོགས་དཔེ་ནི། འདབ། འདི། འདྲ། བ་ལ་རྐྱང་འདོགས་དཔེར་ན།
འབའ། འབྲོག འབྱོར། ཛོ་ལ་རྐྱང་འཕུལ་ནི། འཛེར། འཛུམ།
འཛོལ། ཁ་ལ་རྐྱང་འདོགས། འཁོར། འཁྲུལ། འཁྲི། འཁྱིར།
ཆ་ལ་རྐྱང་འཕུལ། འཆད། འཆང་། འཆར། ཐ་ལ་རྐྱང་འཕུལ།
འཐོབ། ཕ་ལ་རྐྱང་འདོགས། འཕར། འཕྲེང་། འཕྱི། ཚོ་ལ་རྐྱང་
འཕུལ། འཚོལ། ལྟ་བུ། ཤིན་ཏུ་མོ་ཡི་མ་ཡིག་ནི། ཁ་ཆ་ཐ་ཚོ་ག་ཇ
ད། །ཛོང་ཉ་ན་རྣམས་ལ་འཇུག །ཅེས་པ། སྔོན་འཇུག་གི་ཤིན་ཏུ་མོ་མ་ཡིག

ཉེ་མིང་གཞིའི། ཁ་དང་། ཆ་དང་། ཐ་དང་། ཚ་དང་། ག་དང་།
ཇ་དང་། ད་དང་། ཛ་དང་། ང་དང་། ཉ་དང་། ན་བཅས་བཅུ་གཅིག་
ལ་འཇུག་པའི་ཁ་ག་གཉིས་ལ་རྐྱང་འདོགས་དང་། གཞན་མ་རྐྱང་འཕུལ་དཔེར་ན།
མཁའ། མཁྲིས། མཁྱེན། མཆིས། མཐོང་། མཚུངས། མགོན།
མགྲིན། མགྱོགས། མཇལ། མདའ། མཛོད། མངའ། མཉམ།
མནན། ལྟ་བུ། ཇི་ལྟར་འཇུག་པར་བྱེད་ཅེ་ན། ཕོ་ནི་སྒྲ་རྩོལ་དྲག་པར་
འཇུག །མ་ནིང་རན་པར་འཇུག་པ་ཡིན། །མོ་ནི་ཞན་པའི་ཚུལ་གྱིས་ཏེ། །
ཤིན་ཏུ་མོ་ནི་མཉམ་པས་སོ། །ཞེས་པ། སྒྲ་རྩོལ་དང་མཐུན་པའི་སྒོ་ནས་ཇི་ལྟར་
འཇུག་པར་བྱེད་པ་ཡིན་ནམ་ཟེར་ན། སྔོན་འཇུག་གི་ཕོ་བ་ནི་རང་གི་འཇུག་ཡུལ་མིང་
གཞིའི་ཡི་གེ་རྣམས་ལ་སྒྲ་སྐྱེ་སྐད་གདངས་ཆེ་བ་དང་། རྩོལ་བ་ཞེས་པ་དབུགས་ལ་
སོགས་པའི་རྩོལ་བ་ཤིན་ཏུ་ཆེ་བས་སྒྲ་རྩོལ་དྲག་པར་འཇུག་པ་དང་། མ་ནིང་ག་ད་
གཉིས་ནི་སྒྲ་རྩོལ་ཆ་སྙོམས་རན་པ་སྐྱེ་འཚམས་པར་འཇུག་པ་དང་། མོ་འ་ཡིག་ནི་
སྒྲ་རྩོལ་ཞན་པ་སྐྱེ་ཆུང་བའི་ཚུལ་གྱིས་འཇུག་པ་དང་། ཤིན་ཏུ་མོ་མ་ཡིག་ནི་སྒྲ་རྩོལ་
མོ་ལས་ཀྱང་ཤིན་ཏུ་ཞན་པས་ན་མཉམ་པས་སོ་ཞེས་པའོ། །ཅི་ཕྱིར་འཇུག་པར་བྱེད་
ཅེ་ན། ཞེས་པ། སྔོན་འཇུག་ལྔ་པོ་དེ་རྣམས་འཇུག་ཡུལ་མིང་གཞིའི་ཡི་གེ་རྣམས་
ལ་དགོས་པ་ཅི་ཕྱིར་འཇུག་པར་བྱེད་ཅེ་ན། ཐོག་མར་འདི་ལྟར་ཤེས་དགོས་ཏེ། །
ལས་གང་ཞིག་ལ་བྱེད་པ་པོ། །གཞན་དང་དངོས་སུ་འབྲེལ་བ་ཡི། །དབང་དུ་
བྱས་ནས་བྱེད་པོ་དང་། །དེ་ཡི་བྱེད་པ་གཉིས་པོ་ནི། །དངོས་པོ་བདག་ཡིན་བྱ་
ཡུལ་དང་། །བྱ་བ་གཉིས་པོ་དངོས་པོ་གཞན། །ཞེས་པ། སྔོན་འཇུག་གི་ཅི་
ཕྱིར་འཇུག་གི་གཞུང་དོན་ཞིབ་ཏུ་ཤེས་པ་ལ་ཐོག་མར་འདི་ལྟར་ཤེས་པར་བྱེད་དགོས་ཏེ།
ལས་སམ་བྱ་ཡུལ་ལ་བྱ་བ་ཞིག་བྱེད་རྒྱུ་ཡོད་ན་བདག་གཞན་དུས་གསུམ་གྱི་དབྱེ་བ་
འཇུག་ལ། ལས་སམ་བྱ་ཡུལ་ལ་བྱ་བ་བྱེད་རྒྱུ་མེད་ན་བདག་གཞན་དུས་གསུམ་གྱི་
དབྱེ་བ་མི་འཇུག །དེ་ལ་བྱེད་པོ་གཞན་དང་དངོས་སུ་འབྲེལ་བའི་དབང་དུ་བྱས་ནས་
བྱེད་པོ་གང་ཟག་དང་དེའི་བྱེད་པ་ནི་ཤིང་གཅོད་པ་ལྟ་བུར་མཚོན་ན་སྟ་རེ་ཡིན་པས་དེ་

གཉིས་ནི། བདག་གཞན་གཉིས་ཀྱི་ནང་ནས་བདག་ཡིན། དེས་བསྒྲུབ་པར་བྱ་བའི་ཡུལ་གྱི་དངོས་པོ་དང་བྱ་བ་གཉིས་པོ་ནི་བདག་གཞན་གཉིས་ཀྱི་ནང་ནས་གཞན་ཡིན། དེ་ཡང་བྱ་བའི་ཡུལ་གྱི་དངོས་པོ་ནི་ཤིང་ཡིན། བྱ་བ་ནི་ཤིང་གཅོད་པའི་ལས་ཀ་སྟ་རེའི་འདེགས་འཇོག་དང་ཤིང་དུམ་བུར་བཏུབ་པ་སོགས་ཡིན། དཔེར་བརྗོད་ཀྱི་སྐབས་སུ། ཤིང་གཅོད་པ་པོ། ཤིང་གཅོད་པོ། ཞེས་པའི་སྒྲ་འདི་ལྟ་བུས་བྱེད་པོ་གང་ཟག་ཤིང་མཁན་གོ་བས་བདག་གཞན་གཉིས་ནས་བདག་ཡིན། གཅོད་པར་བྱེད། གཅོད་དོ། །ལྟ་བུ་བྱེད་ལས་གསལ་བྱེད་ཀྱི་སྒྲ་ཟེར་བ་ཡིན་ནོ། །དོན་དུ་བྱེད་པ་སྟ་རེ་དང་དེ་འདེགས་པའི་བྱ་བ་གོ་དགོས། བདག་གཞན་གཉིས་ནས་དེ་ཡང་བདག་ཡིན། གཅད་བྱ། གཅད་པར་བྱ་བ། གཅད་བྱའི་ཤིང་། ལྟ་བུ་འདི་རྣམས་ཚིག་བརྗོད་ཚུལ་མི་འདྲ་བ་བྱུང་ཡང་དོན་གཅིག་ཅིང་བྱ་ཡུལ་གསལ་བྱེད་ཀྱི་སྒྲ་ཟེར་བ་ཡིན། འདི་སྐབས་བྱ་ཡུལ་ཤིང་གོ་དགོས་ཤིང་བདག་གཞན་གཉིས་ནས་གཞན་ཡིན། གཅད་པར་བྱ། གཅད་དོ། །ལྟ་བུ་འདི་རྣམས་ལ་བྱ་བའི་ཡུལ་དང་འབྲེལ་བའི་བྱ་བ་གསལ་བྱེད་ཀྱི་སྒྲ་ཟེར་བ་ཡིན། འདི་སྐབས་སྟ་རེ་འདེགས་པའི་བྱ་བ་ཤིང་གི་སྟེང་དུ་བབས་ནས་ཤིང་བཀས་པ་དང་དུམ་བུར་འགྲོ་བ་སོགས་གོ་དགོས་ཤིང་བདག་གཞན་གཉིས་ནས་གཞན་ཡིན། བདག་གཞན་གཉིས་ཀྱི་དབྱེ་བ་དེ་ལྟར་བློ་ལ་བཞག་ནས། དུས་གསུམ་གྱི་དབྱེ་བ་ནི། དེ་བཞིན་བྱེད་པ་པོ་གཞན་དང་། དངོས་སུ་འབྲེལ་མེད་ཇི་ལྟར་ཡང་། བྱ་བ་བྱས་ཟིན་འདས་པ་དང་། བྱ་བ་བྱེད་འགྱུར་མ་འོངས་དང་། བྱེད་བཞིན་པ་ནི་ད་ལྟ་བ། །ཞེས་པ། གོང་དུ་བདག་གཞན་སོ་སོར་དབྱེ་བ་དེ་བཞིན་དུ་བྱེད་པ་པོ་གཞན་དང་དངོས་སུ་འབྲེལ་ཡང་རུང་། མ་འབྲེལ་ཡང་རུང་ཇི་ལྟར་ཡིན་ན་ཡང་། བྱ་བ་བྱས་ཟིན་པ་ནི་འདས་པ་དང་། དཔེར་ན། ལྷ་བསྒྲུབས། ཤིང་བཅད། ལྟ་བུ་དང་། བྱ་བ་བྱེད་འགྱུར་ནི་མ་འོངས་པ་དཔེར་ན། ལྷ་བསྒྲུབ། བསྒྲུབ་པར་བྱ། བསྒྲུབ་བྱ། བསྒྲུབ་པར་བྱ། བསྒྲུབ་བྱའི་ལྷ། གཅད་བྱ། གཅད་པར་བྱ་བ། གཅད་པར་བྱ། གཅད་དོ། །གཅད་བྱའི་ཤིང་། འདི་རྣམས་དུས་གསུམ་ནས་དུས་མ་

འོངས་པ་ཡིན། བྱ་བ་བྱེད་བཞིན་པ་ད་ལྟར་བ་ནི་དཔེར་ན། ལྟ་སྒྲུབ། སྒྲུབ་བོ། སྒྲུབ་བཞིན་པ། སྒྲུབ་གྱིན་འདུག །སྒྲུབ་པར་བྱེད། སྒྲུབ་བྱེད། ཞིང་གཅོད་པར་བྱེད། གཅོད་དོ། །གཅོད་བྱེད། གཅོད་བཞིན་པ། གཅོད་གྱིན་འདུག །ལྟ་བུ་འདི་རྣམས་ད་ལྟ་བ་ཡིན། ཡང་བྱ་བྱེད་ལས་གསུམ་ཟེར་རྒྱུ་འདི་ངོས་འཛིན་ཡག་པོ་ཞིག་དགོས་པས། གཅོད་པོ་དང་། སྒྲུབ་པ་པོ། ལྟ་བུ་འདི་རྣམས་བྱ་བྱེད་ལས་གསུམ་གྱི་ནང་ནས་བྱེད་པ་ཡིན། གཅོད་པར་བྱེད། གཅད་པར་བྱ། གཅད་དོ། སྒྲུབ་པར་བྱེད། བསྒྲུབ་པར་བྱ། བསྒྲུབ་བོ། ལྟ་བུ་བྱ་བྱེད་ལས་གསུམ་གྱི་ནང་ནས་བྱ་བ་ཡིན། གཅད་བྱ། གཅད་པར་བྱ་བ། གཅད་བྱའི་ཤིང་། བསྒྲུབ་བྱ། བསྒྲུབ་པར་བྱ་བ། བསྒྲུབ་བྱའི་ལྷ། ལྟ་བུ་འདི་རྣམས་བྱ་བྱེད་ལས་གསུམ་གྱི་ནང་ནས་ལས་ཟེར་བ་དེ་ཡིན་ཏེ། བསྟན་བཅོས་འདིའི་གཤམ་དུ། ལས་དང་བྱ་ཡུལ་དོན་གཅིག་སྟེ། ཞེས་གསུངས་པའི་ཕྱིར། ཡང་བྱེད་པ་ལ་གཙོ་ཕལ་གཉིས་ཡོད་པས་གཅོད་པ་པོ་ཤིང་གཅོད་མཁན་གང་ཟག་དེ་གཙོ་བོ་ཡིན། གཅོད་བྱེད་སྟ་རེ་ནི་ཕལ་པ་ཡིན། ཤིང་གཅད་པ་བྱ་བ་ཡིན་ཅིང་དེ་ལ་བྱེད་པ་པོ་ལ་ཡོད་པའི་བྱ་བ་དང་། བྱ་བའི་ཡུལ་ལ་ཡོད་པའི་བྱ་བ་གཉིས་ཡོད་དེ། སྟ་རེས་ཤིང་གཅོད་པའི་རྩོལ་བ་ནི་བྱེད་པ་པོ་ཤིང་མཁན་ལ་ཡོད་ཅིང་དེ་གསལ་བྱེད་ཀྱི་སྒྲ་ནི། གཅོད་པར་བྱེད་ཟེར་བ་འདི་ཡིན། ཤིང་དུམ་བུར་བཅད་པའི་ཆ་ནི་བྱ་ཡུལ་ཤིང་གི་སྟེང་དུ་ཡོད་ཅིང་། དེ་གསལ་བྱེད་ཀྱི་སྒྲ་ནི། གཅད་དོ། གཅད་པར་བྱ། ཞེས་པ་འདི་ཡིན་ནོ། །འདི་སྐབས་མཁས་པ་སོ་སོའི་བཞེད་ཚུལ་མི་འདྲ་བ་མང་པོ་འདུག་ཀྱང་རང་ལུགས་འདི་ལྟར་འཐད་པར་སེམས་སོ། །ཡང་གོང་དུ་དངོས་པོ་བདག་ཡིན་ཞེས་པའི་དངོས་པོ་དེ་རྟགས་འཇུག་རྩ་བ་ན་དངོས་སུ་གསུངས་མེད་པས་གསར་བུ་བ་རྣམས་ལ་མ་སྦྱར་ན་རེ་ཞིག་གོ་བདེ་ཞིང་། དངོས་པོ་དང་དངོས་ཅན་གྱི་དངོས་པོ་དེ་ཡིན་ཟེར་བ་གུ་དོག་འབའ་ཞིག་གོ །དེ་ཕྱིར་དུས་གསུམ་དབྱེ་བས་ནི། །བྱེད་ལས་དང་འབྲེལ་ངག་གི་ནི། །སྦྱོར་བ་ཀུན་ལ་ཁྱབ་པ་ཡིན། །ཞེས་པ། རྒྱུ་མཚན་དེའི་ཕྱིར་འདུས་གསུམ་གྱི་དབྱེ་བས་ནི་བྱེད་ལས་དང་

འབྲེལ་བའི་ངག་གི་སྦྱོར་བ་ཐམས་ཅད་ལ་ཁྱབ་པ་ཡིན། ཞེས་པའོ། །དེ་ཡང་གོ་
བདེ་བར་བརྗོད་ན་བྱེད་ལས་དང་འབྲེལ་བའི་ངག་ཡིན་ཚད་ཐམས་ཅད་ཡང་ན་དུས་
འདས་པ་ཡིན་དགོས། ཡང་ན་དུས་མ་འོངས་པ་ཡིན་དགོས། ཡང་ན་ད་ལྟ་བ་
ཡིན་དགོས། ཞེས་པའི་དོན་ནོ། །བདག་གཞན་དབྱེ་བས་དེ་ཙམ་དུ། ཁྱབ་པ་
མིན་ཡང་བྱེད་པོ་དང་། །བྱ་ཡུལ་བསྡུ་ཕྱིར་དབྱེ་བ་དེ། །མཛད་ནས་བདག་གཞན་
དང་འབྲེལ་བའི། །བྱ་བྱེད་རྣམས་ཀྱང་དེ་ཁོངས་བསྡུས། །ཞེས་པ། བདག་
གཞན་གྱི་དབྱེ་བས་བྱེད་ལས་དང་འབྲེལ་བའི་ངག་གི་སྦྱོར་བ་ཐམས་ཅད་ཅད་ལ་དུས་
གསུམ་གྱི་དབྱེ་བས་ཁྱབ་པ་དེ་ཙམ་དུ་མ་ཁྱབ་ཀྱང་། འོ་ན་གང་ལ་མ་ཁྱབ་ཅེ་ན།
གདུགས་སུ་འཁྱེར། ཆུར་འཁྱིལ། ལྟ་བུ་འདི་རྣམས་ལ་དུས་གསུམ་གྱི་དབྱེ་བས་
ཁྱབ་ཀྱང་བདག་གཞན་གྱི་དབྱེ་བས་མ་ཁྱབ་པ་སྟེ་བདག་གཞན་གྱི་དབྱེ་བའི་ཁོངས་སུ་མ་
གཏོགས་སོ། །བདག་གཞན་གྱི་དབྱེ་བ་མཛད་པའི་དགོས་པ་ནི། སྒྲུབ་པ་པོ།
བསྒྲུབ་བྱའི་ལྟ། ལྟ་བུ་བྱེད་པ་པོ་དང་བྱ་ཡུལ་གཉིས་བསྡུ་བའི་ཕྱིར་དུ་དབྱེ་བ་དེ་
མཛད་ནས། དེའི་ཞར་ལ་བདག་གཞན་དང་འབྲེལ་བའི་བྱ་བྱེད་ཀྱི་ཚིག་ཕན་ཚུན་ཤེད་
མཚུངས་པ་རྣམས་ཀྱང་དེ་ཁོངས་བསྡུས་ཞེས་པའོ། །བྱ་བྱེད་ཀྱི་སྒྲ་ཤེད་མཚུངས་
བདག་གཞན་གྱི་ཁོངས་སུ་བསྡུ་ཚུལ་ཇི་ལྟར་ཡིན་སྙམ་ན། སྒྲུབ་པར་བྱེད། ཅེས་
པའི་ཚིག་འདི་སྒྲུབ་པ་པོ་ཞེས་པ་དང་ཤེད་མཚུངས་ཡིན་པས་བདག་གཞན་གཉིས་ཀྱི་
ནང་ནས་བདག་གི་ཁོངས་སུ་བསྡུས། བསྒྲུབ་པར་བྱ། ཞེས་པ་འདི་བསྒྲུབ་བྱའི་
ལྟ་ཞེས་པ་དང་ཤེད་མཚུངས་ཡིན་པས་བདག་གཞན་གཉིས་ཀྱི་ནང་ནས་གཞན་གྱི་
ཁོངས་སུ་བསྡུས། །ཡང་བདག་གཞན་གྱི་དབྱེ་བ་མ་མཛད་ན་ཅིར་འགྱུར་སྙམ་ན།
མ་མཛད་ན་སྐྱོན་འདི་ལྟར། དཔེར་ན། སྐལ་ལྡན་གྱིས་སངས་རྒྱས་བསྒྲུབས་ལྟ་
བུའི་ཚེ། བསྒྲུབས་ཞེས་པའི་ཚིག་ཁོ་ནས་དུས་འདས་པ་གོ་ནུས་ཀྱང་། སྐལ་
ལྡན་དང་སངས་རྒྱས་དེ་ཇི་ལྟ་བུ་ཡིན་ནམ་སྙམ་དོགས་པ་འབྱུང་བའི་སྐྱོན་ཡོད།
བདག་གཞན་གྱི་དབྱེ་བ་མཛད་པས་སྐལ་ལྡན་དེ་བདག་བྱེད་པོ་དང་། སངས་རྒྱས་
བསྒྲུབས་པར་བྱ་བ་གཞན་དེ་ཡིན་པ་བདེ་བླག་ཏུ་གོ་བའི་དགོས་པ་ཡོད་པས་དེའི་ཕྱིར་

བདག་གཞན་གྱི་དབྱེ་བ་མཛད་དོ། །དེས་ན་དུས་གསུམ་དུ་དབྱེ་བ། །བདག་
གཞན་དབྱེ་བས་མ་ཁྱབ་པ། །བསྡུ་བའི་དོན་དུ་ཤེས་དགོས་པར། །གསུངས་ཀྱང་
སྔོན་འཇུག་འ་ཡིག་སྐབས། །བྱེད་ལས་ཙམ་དང་འབྲེལ་བ་ཡི། །དངོས་པོ་
བདག་ལའང་འཇུག་པ་མཐོང་། །ཞེས་པ། དེས་ན་འདས་པ། མ་འོངས་པ།
ད་ལྟ་བ་བཅས་དུས་གསུམ་དུ་དབྱེ་བའི་དགོས་པ་ནི། བདག་གཞན་གྱི་དབྱེ་བས་མ་
ཁྱབ་པའམ་མ་བསྡུས་པ་ལྟུགས་གསེར་དུ་གྱུར་ལྟ་བུ་དུས་འདས་པ་དང་། ཀྱུ་འཁྱིལ་
བར་འགྱུར་ལྟ་བུ་དུས་མ་འོངས་པ་དང་། གདུགས་འཁྱིལ་གྱིན་འདུག །འཁྱིར་
བཞིན་པའོ། ལྟ་བུ་དུས་ད་ལྟ་བ་རྣམས་སུ་བསྡུ་བའི་དོན་དུ་ཤེས་དགོས་པར་
གསུངས་ཀྱང་སྔོན་འཇུག་འ་ཡིག་སྐབས་བྱེད་ལས་ཙམ་དང་འབྲེལ་བ་ཡི། ཆོས་
འཆད་པ་པོ། འཆད་པར་བྱེད། ལྟ་བུ་དངོས་པོ་བདག་ལའང་འཇུག་པ་མཐོང་
ངོ་། །ཞེས་པའོ། །དེ་ལྟར་ངེས་ནས་ཕོ་ཡིག་བ། །ཞེས་པ། བཤད་མ་ཐག
པ་དེ་ལྟར་ཚུལ་བཞིན་ངེས་ནས་སྔོན་འཇུག་གི་ཕོ་ཡིག་བ་ནི། དུས་འདས་པ་དང་།
གཞན་གཉིས་ལ་འཇུག་པའི་དཔེར་བརྗོད་ནི། ཞེས་པའོ། །བསྒྲུབས་སོ་ལྟ་བུ་
འདས་པ་དང་། །ཞེས་པ། བསྒྲུབས་སོ། བཀང་། བཅད། ལྟ་བུ་འདི་
རྣམས་དུས་འདས་པ་ཡིན་པས་དེས་མཚོན་ནས་རྒྱ་ཆེར་ཤེར་པར་བྱའོ། །བསྒྲུབ་བྱའི་
ལྟ་དང་བསྒྲུབ་པར་བྱ། །ཞེས་སོགས་དངོས་པོ་གཞན་ལ་འཇུག །ཅེས་པ།
ཕོ་ཡིག་བསྒྲུབ་བྱའི་ལྟ་སོགས་དངོས་པོ་གཞན་ལ་འཇུག་པའི་དཔེ་ནི། བསྒྲུབ་བྱ།
བསྒྲུབ་པར་བྱ་བ། བསྒྲུབ་བྱའི་ལྟ། བཅག་བྱ། བཅག་པར་བྱ། བཅག་
བྱའི་ཇོ། ལྟ་བུ། །མ་ནིང་ག་ད་གཉིས་པོ་ནི། །ཞེས་པ། སྔོན་འཇུག་མ་
ནིང་ག་དང་ད་གཉིས་པོ་ནི་དངོས་པོ་བདག་དང་། དངོས་པོ་གཞན་དང་། དུས་ད་
ལྟ་བ་བཅས་གསུམ་ལ་འཇུག་པ་ལས་དང་པོ་དངོས་པོ་བདག་ལ་འཇུག་པ་ནི། །
གཅོད་པ་པོ་དང་གཅོད་པར་བྱེད། །གཅོད་པར་འགྱུར་དང་དཀྲི་བ་པོ། །དཀྲི་བར་
བྱེད་དང་དཀྲི་བར་འགྱུར། །ཞེས་སོགས་དངོས་པོ་བདག་དོན་དང་། །ཞེས་པ།
ཤིང་གཅོད་པ་པོ། གཅོད་བྱེད། གཅོད་པར་བྱེད། གཅོད་པར་འགྱུར་རོ།

སྣལ་མ་དཀྲི་བ་པོ། དཀྲི་བར་བྱེད། དཀྲི་བར་འགྱུར། གསོད་པ་པོ།
གསོད་པར་བྱེད། རྒྱ་མཚོ་དཀྲུག་པ་པོ། དཀྲུག་པར་བྱེད། ལྟ་བུ་དངོས་པོ་
བདག་གསལ་བྱེད་ཀྱི་དོན་དུ་གོ་བར་བྱའོ། །གཉིས་པ། །གཅད་བྱའི་ཤིང་དང་
གཅད་པར་བྱ། །དཀྲི་བྱའི་སྣལ་མ་དཀྲི་བར་བྱ། །ཞེས་སོགས་དངོས་པོ་གཞན་
དོན་དང་། །ཞེས་པ། མ་ནིང་ག་ད་གཉིས་གཅད་བྱའི་ཤིང་སོགས་དངོས་པོ་
གཞན་དོན་དུ་འཇུག་པ་ནི། གསད་བྱ། གསད་པར་བྱ་བ། གསད་བྱའི་ལུག
དགག་བྱ། དགག་པར་བྱ་བ། དགག་བྱའི་སྐྱོན། ལྟ་བུ་གསུམ། གཅོད་
བཞིན་པ་དང་དཀྲི་བཞིན་པ། །ཞེས་སོགས་ད་ལྟ་སྒྲུབ་ཆེད་འཇུག །ཅེས་པ།
མ་ནིང་ག་ད་གཉིས་བྱེད་པ་པོ་གཞན་དང་དངོས་སུ་འབྲེལ་བའི་བྱ་བ་བྱེད་བཞིན་པ་ད་ལྟ་
བར་འཇུག་པ་ནི། ཤིང་གཅོད་བཞིན་པ། གཅོད་ཀྱིན་འདུག སྣལ་མ་དཀྲི་
བཞིན་པ། དཀྲི་ཡིན་འདུག །དོན་གཉེར་བཞིན་པ། གཉེར་གྱིན་འདུག །
ཞོ་དཀྲོག་བཞིན་པ། དཀྲོག་པའི་སྐབས་ཡིན། ལྟ་བུ་བྱེད་ལས་གསལ་བྱེད་ཀྱི་སྒྲ་
ཚིག་གྲོགས་ཀྱིས་བསྒྱུར་པ་འདི་རྣམས་ད་ལྟ་བ་བསྒྲུབ་པའི་ཆེད་དུ་འཇུག་གོ། །མོ་
ཡིག་འ་ནི་བདག་དངོས་དང་། བདག་དོན་ཕལ་པ་དང་། དུས་ད་ལྟ་བ་དང་།
མ་འོངས་པ་བཅས་བཞི་ལ་འཇུག །དང་པོ་བདག་དངོས་ནི། མོ་ཡིག་འ་ནི་
འཆད་པ་པོ། །འཆད་པར་བྱེད་དང་འཆད་པར་འགྱུར། །ཞེས་སོགས་དངོས་པོ་
བདག་དངོས་དང་། ཞེས་པ། ཆོས་འཆད་པ་པོ། འཆད་པར་བྱེད།
འཆད་པར་འགྱུར། མདུད་པ་འགྲོལ་བ་པོ། འགྲོལ་བྱེད། འགྲོལ་བར་
འགྱུར། དེ་སོགས་དངོས་པོ་བདག་ཡིན་པས་དེ་བསྒྲུབ་པའི་ཕྱིར་འཇུག་གོ
།གཉིས་པ་བདག་དོན་ཕལ་པ་ནི། །འགྲོ་བ་པོ་དང་འགྲོ་བར་བྱེད། །ཅེས་སོགས་
བདག་དོན་ཕལ་པ་དང་། །ཞེས་པ། མོ་ཡིག་བདག་དོན་ཕལ་པ་ལ་འཇུག་པའི་
དཔེ་ནི། གང་དུ་འགྲོ་བ་པོ། འགྲོ་བར་བྱེད། འགྲོ་བར་འགྱུར་རོ། །མགོ་
འཁོར་བ་པོ། འཁོར་བྱེད། ཕྱོགས་ཤར་ནས་འཆར་བ་པོ། འཆར་བྱེད།
འོད་འཚེར་བ་པོ། འཚེར་བྱེད། སོགས་བྱ་བྱེད་ངོ་བོ་གཅིག་པའམ་ཐ་མི་དད་པར་

སྣང་བའི་བདག་དོན་ཐལ་པ་ལ་འཇུག་པའོ། །གསུམ་པ་དུས་ད་ལྟ་བ་ནི། །འཁྲོལ་ལོ་ཞེས་སོགས་ད་ལྟ་བ། །ཞེས་པ། ཆུ་འཁྲོལ་ལོ། །འཁྲོལ་བཞིན་པ། གདན་ལ་འཁོད་བཞིན་པ། འཁོད་མུས་ཡིན། མེ་འབར་བཞིན་པ། བདེ་བར་འཚོ་བཞིན་པ། སོགས་བདག་གཞན་གྱི་དབྱེ་བས་མ་བསྡུས་པའི་དུས་ད་ལྟ་བ་བསྒྲུབ་པའི་ཕྱིར་འཇུག་པའོ། །བཞི་པ་དུས་མ་འོངས་པ་ནི། །འཁྲོལ་བར་འགྱུར་སོགས་མ་འོངས་འཇུག །ཅེས་པ། ཆུ་འཁྲོལ་བར་འགྱུར། སྨན་འཇུ་བར་འགྱུར། ལུས་འཚོ་བར་འགྱུར། དེ་ལ་སོགས་པ་བྱ་བྱེད་ཐ་མི་དད་དུ་སྣང་བའི་བྱ་བ་བྱེད་འགྱུར་མ་འོངས་པ་བསྒྲུབ་པའི་ཕྱིར་འཇུག་གོ །ཤིན་ཏུ་མོ་ཡི་མ་ཡིག་ནི། །བདག་གཞན་དུས་གསུམ་མཉམ་པར་འཇུག །ཅེས་པ་སྔོན་འཇུག་གི་ཤིན་ཏུ་མོ་མ་ཡིག་ནི་བདག་གཞན་གཉིས་དང་དུས་གསུམ་སྤྱི་ཐམས་ཅད་ལ་མཉམ་པར་འཇུག །དེ་ཡང་བདག་ལ་འཇུག་པ་ནི། མཁྱེན་པ་པོ། མཁས་པར་བྱེད། ལྟ་བུ། གཞན་ལ། འཇུག་པ་ནི། མཁས་བྱ། མཆོད་བྱ། མཆོད་པར་བྱ། ལྟ་བུ། དུས་འདས་པ་ལ་འཇུག་པ་ནི། མཁྱེན་ཏོ། །མཁས་པར་བྱས། མགུ་བར་བྱས། ལྟ་བུ། དུས་ད་ལྟ་བར་འཇུག་པ་ནི། མཁྱེན་བཞིན་པ། མཛལ་བཞིན་པ། མཐུན་གྱིན་འདུག །ལྟ་བུ། མ་འོངས་པ་ལ་འཇུག་པ་ནི། མཁས་པར་འགྱུར། མཛའ་བར་འགྱུར། མཐུན་པར་འགྱུར། ལྟ་བུ་ཀུན་ལ་མཉམ་པར་འཇུག་གོ །འོན་ཀྱང་བྱེད་པོ་གཞན་དངོས་དང་། འབྲེལ་བའི་འདས་ལ་འའི་སྔོན་འཇུག །མེད་པར་ངེས་ཤིང་གད་ཅུང་། །ཞེས་པ། འོན་ཀྱང་བྱེད་པོ་གཞན་དང་དངོས་སུ་འབྲེལ་བའི་འདས་ཚིག་རྣམས་ལ་འའི་སྔོན་འཇུག་མེད་པར་ངེས་ཤིང་། དེར་མ་ཟད་ག་ད་གཉིས་ཀྱང་ཅུང་བར་ཡོད་དོ་ཞེས་པའོ། །ད་ལྟ་བ་ལ་བའི་སྔོན་འཇུག ཅུང་ཞིང་མགོ་ཅན་ད་ལྟ་བར། བས་འཕུལ་མེད་པར་ངེས་པ་ཙམ། ཞེས་པ། ད་ལྟ་བའི་ཚིག་རྣམས་ལ་བ་ཡིག་གི་སྔོན་འཇུག་ཅུང་བར་མ་ཟད། ར་ལ་སའི་མགོ་ཅན་ད་ལྟ་བ་རྣམས་ལ་ཡང་བ་འཕུལ་མེད་པར་ངེས་པ་ཙམ་ཡིན། ཞེས་པའོ། །གཞན་ཡང་བས་འཕུལ་ཅན་ཐལ་ཆེར། བྱེད་པ་པོ་ནི་ད་ལྟ་དང་།

བྱ་ཡུལ་མ་འོངས་པར་བསྡུས་ནས། །ཞེས་པ། གཞན་ཡང་བའི་འཕྲུལ་བརྟེན་ཅན་ཕལ་ཆེར་བྱེད་པ་པོ་དང་། བྱ་ཡུལ་གཉིས་ལས་བྱེད་པ་པོ་ནི་ད་ལྟ་བའི་ཁོངས་དང་། བྱ་ཡུལ་མ་འོངས་པའི་ཁོངས་སུ་བསྡུས་ནས་དུས་འདས་པ་དང་། ད་ལྟ་བ་དང་། མ་འོངས་པ་དང་། བསྐུལ་ཚིག་བཅས་བཞི་རུ་དབྱེ་བར་བྱའོ། །དང་པོ་ནི། འདས་ལ་བས་འཕྲུལ་ཡང་འཇུག་ཡོད། །ཅེས་པ། མགོ་ཅན་འདས་ཚིག་རྣམས་ལ་བ་སོགས་སྔོན་འཇུག་དང་ཡང་འཇུག་གཉིས་ཀ་འཇུག་སྟེ། དཔེར་ན། ལྟ་བསྒོམས། ལྟ་བུ། གཉིས་པ་ནི། །ད་ལྟ་བ་ལ་གཉིས་ཀ་མེད། །ཅེས་པ། ད་ལྟ་བའི་ཚིག་རྣམས་ལ་སྔོན་འཇུག་ཡང་འཇུག་གང་ཡང་མི་འཇུག་པའི་དཔེ་ནི། སྒྲུབ་པ་པོ། སྒྲུབ་བྱེད། སྒྲུབ་པར་བྱེད། སྒྲུབ་པོ། ལྟ་བུ། གསུམ་པ་ནི། །མ་འོངས་འཕྲུལ་ཡོད་ཡང་འཇུག་མེད། །ཅེས་པ། མ་འོངས་པའི་ཚིག་རྣམས་ལ་འཕྲུལ་ཡོད་ཡང་འཇུག་མེད་པའི་དཔེ་ནི། བསྒྲུབ་བྱ། བསྒྲུབ་པར་བྱ། བསྒྲུབ་བྱའི་ལྟ། ལྟ་བུ། བཞི་པ་བསྐུལ་ཚིག་རྣམས་ལ་ཡང་འཇུག་ཡོད་མེད་གཉིས། དང་པོ་ཡོད་པ་ནི། །བསྐུལ་ཚིག་འཕྲུལ་མེད་ཡང་འཇུག་ཡོད། །ཅེས་པ། བསྐུལ་ཚིག་རྣམས་ལ་འཕྲུལ་བརྟེན་སྔོན་འཇུག་མེད་ཅིང་། ཡང་འཇུག་ཡོད་པའི་དཔེ་ནི། སྒྲུབས་ཤིག སྡུངས་ཤིག ལྟ་བུ། གཉིས་པ་ཡང་འཇུག་མེད་པ་ནི། །སྐབས་འགར་འདས་དང་བསྐུལ་ཚིག་ལ། །ས་རྒྱུད་སྦྱར་བས་ཐུས་པའང་ཡོད། །ཅེས་པ། འདས་ཚིག་དང་བསྐུལ་ཚིག་ཕལ་ཆེར་ལ་ཡང་འཇུག་ཐོབ་ཀྱང་། སྐབས་འགར་འདས་པ་དང་བསྐུལ་ཚིག་གཉིས་ལ་ས་རྒྱུད་སྦྱར་བས་ཐུས་པ་སྟེ་ཚོག་པའང་ཡོད་དེ། འདས་པ་ལ་ས་རྒྱུད་སྦྱར་བས་ཐུས་པ་ནི། བྱས། འདས། བལྟས། ལྟ་བུ། བསྐུལ་ཚིག་ལ་ས་རྒྱུད་སྦྱར་བས་ཐུས་པ་ནི། གྱིས་ཤིག ལྟོས་ཤིག སྐུས། ལྟ་བུ། །རྗེས་འཇུག་ཡི་གེ་བཅུ་པོ་ཡི། །ག་ད་བ་ས་བཞི་རྣམས་ཕོ། །ང་མ་འ་གསུམ་མོ་ཡིན་ཅིང་། །ན་ར་ལ་གསུམ་མ་ནིང་སྟེ། །མིང་གཞིའི་ཡི་གེ་ཀུན་ལ་འཇུག །ཅེས་པ། རྗེས་འཇུག་གི་རྟགས་ཀྱི་དབྱེ་བ་བཤད་པ་སྟེ། ག་ང་ད་ན་བ་མ་འ། ར་ལ་ས་རྣམས་རྗེས་

འཇུག་བཅུ། ཞེས་པ་ལྟར་རྗེས་འཇུག་ཡི་གེ་བཅུ་པོ་དེ་རྣམས་ལ་ནང་གསེས་དབྱེ་ན་གསུམ་དུ་ཡོད། གསུམ་གང་ཞེ་ན། ཕོ་དང་། མོ་དང་། མ་ནིང་སྟེ་གསུམ་དུ་འགྱུར་རོ། །དང་པོ་ནི། ག་དང་། ད་དང་། བ་དང་། ས་བཅས་བཞི་ནི་ཕོ་ཡིག་གོ། །གཉིས་པ། ང་དང་། མ་དང་། འ་བཅས་གསུམ་ནི་མོ་ཡིག་གོ །གསུམ་པ། ན་དང་། ར་དང་། ལ་བཅས་གསུམ་ནི་མ་ནིང་གི་ཡི་གེའོ། །དེ་རྣམས་མིང་གཞིའི་ཡི་གེ་ཀུན་ལ་འཇུག་པ་ཡིན་ནོ། །ཞེས་པའོ། ཇི་ལྟར་འཇུག་ཚུལ་གཉིས་ཡིན་ཏེ། ཞེས་པ། རྗེས་འཇུག་གི་རྟགས་ཀྱི་འཇུག་ཚུལ་བཤད་པ་སྟེ་རྗེས་འཇུག་རྣམས་ཇི་ལྟར་འཇུག་པའི་ཚུལ་ལ་གཉིས་ཡོད་པ་ཡིན་ཏེ། སྒྲའི་འཇུག་ཚུལ་དང་། དོན་གྱི་འཇུག་ཚུལ་གཉིས་ལས་དང་པོ་ནི། དང་པོ་སྒྲ་ཡི་འཇུག་ཚུལ་ནི། །ཞེས་པ། དང་པོ་སྒྲ་ཡི་འཇུག་ཚུལ་དེ་ལ་ཡང་རྗེས་འཇུག་ཕོ་གསུམ་ནི་མིང་གཞིའི་ཡི་གེ་གང་ལ་ཞུགས་ཀྱང་བརྗོད་པའི་སྒྲ་གདངས་དྲག་པར་འཇུག་པ་དང་། མོ་གཉིས་ནི་སྒྲ་གདངས་ཞན་པར་འཇུག་པ་དང་། མ་ནིང་གསུམ་ནི་བར་མ་སྟེ་སྒྲ་གདངས་རན་པར་འཇུག་པ་ཡིན་ནོ། །ཕོ་ལ་ཡང་ནང་གསེས་སྒྲ་རྩོལ་དྲག་པ་རྣམས་སྐྱེས་བུ་རབ་དང་། དེ་ལས་ཅུང་ཟད་ཞན་པ་བར་མ་རྣམས་སྐྱེས་བུ་འབྲིང་དང་། དེ་ལས་ཀྱང་ཤིན་ཏུ་ཞན་པ་སྐྱེས་བུ་ཐ་མ་སྟེ་གསུམ་དུ་ཡོད་པའི་དང་པོ་ནི། །ཕོ་ཡི་ག་ཡིག་ཡང་འཇུག་ཅན། །སྐྱེས་བུ་རབ་དང་། ཞེས་པ། རྗེས་འཇུག་གི་ཕོ་ག་ཡིག་ལ་ཡང་འཇུག་ས་ཞུགས་ན་སྐྱེས་བུ་རབ་ཡིན་ཏེ། དཔེར་ན། མདོ་བསྒྲགས། དོན་གཟིགས། ལྟ་བུ་དང་། ཕོ་ཡིག་བ། ཡང་འཇུག་ཅན་རྣམས་སྐྱེས་བུ་འབྲིང་། །ཞེས་པ། ཕོ་ཡིག་བ་ཡང་འཇུག་དང་འབྲེལ་ན་སྐྱེས་བུ་འབྲིང་ཡིན་ཏེ། དཔེར་ན། སྐྱབས། བསྒྲུབས། སྟོབས། ལྟ་བུའོ། །ག་བ་ཡང་འཇུག་མེད་པ་དང་། ད་སའི་མཐའ་ཅན་ཐ་མ་སྟེ། །ཞེས་པ། ག་དང་བ་གཉིས་ཡང་འཇུག་མེད་པ་དང་། ད་སའི་མཐའ་ཅན་ཏེ་ད་དང་ས་རྗེས་འཇུག་ཏུ་ཡོད་པ་རྣམས་སྐྱེས་བུ་ཐ་མ་ཡིན་ཏེ། དཔེར་ན། བདག མཆོག །ཁབ། དབ། ཡོད། བསྟོད། སྐྱེས། བཞེས། ལྟ་བུའོ། །དྲག་

པ་པོ་ལའང་ནང་གསེས་གྱིས། དྲག་ཞན་བར་མ་གསུམ་དུ་དབྱེ། །ཞེས་པ། དྲག་པ་པོའི་ཡི་གེ་ལའང་ནང་གསེས་ཀྱིས་དྲག་པ་སྐྱེས་བུ་རབ་དང་། བར་མ་སྐྱེས་བུ་འབྲིང་དང་། ཞན་པ་སྐྱེས་བུ་ཐ་མ་སྟེ་བཤད་མ་ཐག་པ་བཞིན་གསུམ་དུ་འགྱུར་རོ། །དེ་བཞིན་ཞན་པ་མོ་ལ་ཡང་། ནང་གསེས་དྲག་ཞན་གཉིས་དབྱེ་སྟེ། ། ཞེས་པ། ཕོ་ལ་སྐྱེས་བུ་གསུམ་དུ་དབྱེ་བ་དེ་བཞིན་དུ་ཞན་པ་མོ་ལ་ཡང་ནང་གསེས་དྲག་པ་མོ་དང་། །ཞན་པ་ཤིན་ཏུ་མོ་སྟེ་གཉིས་སུ་དབྱེ་སྟེ། ང་མ་ཡང་འཇུག་ཅན་མོ་དང་། །ཞེས་པ། ང་དང་། མ་གཉིས་ཡང་འཇུག་ཅན་རྣམས་དྲག་པ་མོ་ཙམ་ཡིན་ཏེ། དཔེར་ན། བཞེངས། གངས། དབྱིངས། བྲམས། བསྒོམས། རྣམས། ལྷ་བུའོ། །གཉིས་པ། ང་མ་ཡང་འཇུག་མེད་པ་དང་། །འ་མཐའ་ཅན་རྣམས་ཤིན་ཏུ་མོ། །ཞེས་པ། ང་དང་མ་གཉིས་ཡང་འཇུག་མེད་པ་དང་། འ་དང་བཅས་གསུམ་པོ་རྣམས་ཀྱི་མཐའ་ཅན་ཏེ་རྗེས་འཇུག་ནི་ཤིན་ཏུ་མོ་ཡིན་པའི་དཔེ་ནི། མཐོང་། ཞིང་། གསུམ། གཏམ། བཀའ། དགའ། མཁའ། མདའ། ལྷ་བུའོ། །བར་མ་མ་ནིང་ན་ར་ལ། །ཡང་འཇུག་ཡོད་དམ་མེད་ཀྱང་རུང་། །མིང་གཞི་ཕོ་ཡིག་མཐར་ཡོད་དང་། མིང་གཞི་མ་ནིང་རྗེས་སུ་ནི། ཡང་འཇུག་དང་བཅས་ཞུགས་པ་ན། དྲག་དང་འཐྲད་པས་དྲག་པར་འགྱུར། །ཞེས་པ། སྒྲ་གདངས་བར་མ་མ་ནིང་ན་ར་ལ་གསུམ་པོ་འདི་ལ་ཡང་འཇུག་ཡོད་དམ་མེད་ཀྱང་རུང་མིང་གཞི་ཕོ་ཡིག་གི་མཐར་ཡོད་པ་དང་། མིང་གཞི་མ་ནིང་གི་རྗེས་སུ་ཡང་འཇུག་དང་བཅས་ཏེ་ཞུགས་པ་ན་སྒྲ་གདངས་དྲག་པ་དང་འཐྲད་པ་ཡིན་པས་དྲག་པར་འགྱུར་ཏེ། དཔེར་ན་མིང་གཞི་ཕོ་ཡིག་དང་འཐྲད་པ་ནི། ཀུན། དཀོན། བཀར། བཀོལ། སྐྱོལ། ཅན། གཅེརད། བཙོལད། གཏན། བསྣནད། དཔོན། སྤར། དཔལ། སྤེལད། བརྩོན། བཙིརད། སྤུལད། སོགས་སོ། མིང་གཞི་མ་ནིང་གི་རྗེས་སུ་ཡང་འཇུག་དང་བཅས་ཞུགས་པ་ན། འཕོནད། ཆརད། ཐརད། ཕུལད། ཚོརད། ལྷ་བུ་དྲག་དང་འཐྲད་པས་དྲག་པར་འགྱུར་

བའོ། །འདི་སྐབས་སི་དཏུལ་གཉིས་ཙུང་མི་འདྲ་བ་འདུག །མིང་གཞི་མོ་ཡིག་
རྗེས་སུ་ནི། །ཡང་འཇུག་མེད་པར་ཞུགས་པ་ན། །ཞན་དང་འཕྲད་པས་ཞན་པར་
འགྱུར། །ཞེས་པ། ན་ར་ལ་གསུམ་མིང་གཞི་མོ་ཡིག་གི་རྗེས་སུ་ནི་ཡང་འཇུག་
མེད་པར་ཞུགས་པ་ན་ཞན་དང་འཕྲད་པས་ཞན་པར་འགྱུར་ཏེ། དཔེར་ན། འགྲན།
འགོར། མགུལ། ལྐོན། འཇུར། མཇལ། དོན། འབར།
འཛུལ། གཞོན། ཟུར། འོལ། གཡོན། བཞོར། གསལ།
སོགས་སོ། །དེ་གཉིས་འགྱུར་བ་མ་ཉིད་ཡིན། །ཞེས་པ། གོང་གི་དྲག་ཞན་
གཉིས་པོ་དེ་འགྱུར་བ་མ་ཉིད་སྟེ་འགྱུར་བ་ཞེས་པའི་དོན་ནི་མིང་གཞི་དྲག་པ་དང་འཕྲད་
ན་དྲག་པ་དང་། མིང་གཞི་ཞན་པ་དང་འཕྲད་ན་ཞན་པར་འགྱུར་བ་སྟེ་རང་གསོ་མི་
ཟིན་པས་ན་འགྱུར་བ་ཞེས་བརྗོད་པ་ཡིན་ནོ། །མིང་གཞི་མོ་ཡིག་རྗེས་སུ་ནི། །
ཡང་འཇུག་དང་བཅས་ཞུགས་པ་ན། །དྲག་ཞན་གཉིས་ཀའི་ཆ་ལྡན་ཕྱིར། །
མཚན་གཉིས་མ་ཉིད་ཞེས་སུ་གྲགས། །ཞེས་པ། ན་ར་ལ་གསུམ་མིང་གཞི་མོ་
ཡིག་གི་རྗེས་སུ་ཡང་འཇུག་དང་བཅས་ཏེ་ཞུགས་པ་ན་དྲག་ཞན་གཉིས་ཀའི་ཆ་དང་ལྡན་
པའི་ཕྱིར། མཚན་གཉིས་མ་ཉིད་ཞེས་གྲགས་པ་ཡིན་ཏེ། དཔེར་ན།
བསྐྲརད། བརྐྱལད། འཇལད། དོནད། དབེནད། འཛེརད།
བཞརད། ཟེནད། ཟུརད། འོནད། གཡུལད། ཤརད། གསོལད།
ལྟ་བུ་མིང་གཞི་མོ་ཡིག་དང་འཕྲད་པས་མོའི་ཆ་དང་ལྡན། ཡང་འཇུག་ཕོ་ཡིག་དང་
འཕྲད་པས་ཕོའི་ཆ་དང་ལྡན་པས་མཚན་གཉིས་དང་། རྗེས་འཇུག་ཁོ་རང་མ་ཉིད་
ཡིན་པས་མཚན་གཉིས་མ་ཉིད་ཞེས་བརྗོད་དོ། །མིང་གཞི་མ་ཉིད་རྗེས་སུ་ནི། །
ཡང་འཇུག་མེད་པར་ཞུགས་པ་ན། །དྲག་ཞན་གང་དུའང་མི་འགྱུར་བས། །
མཚན་མེད་མ་ཉིད་ཞེས་སུ་འདོད། །ཅེས་པ། མིང་གཞི་མ་ཉིད་ཁ་ཆ་ཐ་ཕ་ཚ་
ལྟའི་རྗེས་སུ་ནི་ཡང་འཇུག་མེད་པར་ཞུགས་པ་ན་དྲག་ཞན་གང་དུ་འང་མི་འགྱུར་ཏེ།
དཔེར་ན། མཁན། འཁོར། ཁལ། ཆེན། འཆར། འཆལ།
མཐུན། ཐུར། འཐོལ། ཕན། འཕུར། འཕེལ། ཚོན། ཚུར།

འཚོལ། ལྷ་བུ་མིང་གཞི་དང་རྗེས་འཇུག་གཉིས་ཀ་མ་ཉིད་ཡིན་ཅིང་ཕོ་མོའི་མཚན་
མ་གང་ཡང་མེད་པས་མཚན་མེད་མ་ཉིད་ཞེས་སུ་འདོད་དོ། །གཉིས་པ་ནི། །
གཉིས་པ་དོན་ལ་གཉིས་ཡོད་པའི། །ཞེས་པ། གཉིས་པ་དོན་གྱི་འཇུག་ཚུལ་
བཤད་པ་ལ་གཉིས། སྔ་མ་གང་ལྟར་གྱུར་བ་བཤད་པ་དང༌། ཕྱི་མ་གང་ལྟར་
འགྱུར་པ་བཤད་པའོ། །དང་པོ་ནི། །སྔ་མ་གང་ལྟར་གྱུར་བ་ནི། །རྗེས་འཇུག
གང་ལ་ཞུགས་པ་ཡི། །མིང་དེས་བདག་གཞན་སོགས་གང་སྟོན། །ཞེས་པ།
རྗེས་འཇུག་དེ་རྣམས་གང་ལ་ཞུགས་པའི་མིང་དེ་ཉིད་མིང་མཐའ་སོགས་ལ་ལྟོས་ནས་
སྔ་མར་གྲུབ་པ་ཡིན་པས་དེས་བདག་གཞན་སོགས་གང་དང་གང་སྟོན་པ་ནི། །ཕལ་
ཆེར་མིང་དེའི་སྟོན་འཇུག་གི །ནུས་པར་སྦྱར་ནས་རྟོགས་པར་བྱ། ཞེས་པ།
མིང་དེས་དོན་གང་སྟོན་པ་ཕལ་ཆེར་མིང་དེའི་སྟོན་འཇུག་ལྔ་ལས་གང་ཞིག་ཡིན་པ་དེའི་
ནུས་པར་སྦྱར་ནས་བདག་གཞན་དུས་གསུམ་སོགས་གང་ཡིན་རྟོགས་པར་བྱ་དགོས་ཏེ།
དཔེར་ན། རྗེས་འཇུག་ཕོ་བཞི་ཅི་རིགས་པར་དུས་འདས་པ་ལ་འཇུག་པ།
བསྒྲིགས། བསྒྲུབས། བཀག བཏབ། བཤད། བརྟས། ལྟ་བུ།
བདག་ལ་འཇུག་པ་ནི། འགྲོགས་བྱེད། འདེབས་བྱེད། འགོག་བྱེད།
སྒྲུབ་བྱེད། སྟུད་བྱེད། མཛེས་བྱེད། ལྟ་བུ་དང༌། དེ་རྣམས་གཞན་ལ་
འཇུག་པ་ནི། གདགས་བྱ། དགག་བྱ། བསྒྲུབ་བྱ། བརྗོད་བྱ། ལྟ་བུ་
དང༌། བདག་གཞན་གྱི་དབྱེ་བས་མ་བསྡུས་པའི་དུས་ད་ལྟ་བར་འཇུག་པ་ནི།
འཕགས་བཞིན་པ། འཇུག་བཞིན་པ། འགྲུབ་བཞིན་པ། འཕོད་བཞིན་པ།
དགྲེས་བཞིན་པ། དུས་མ་འོངས་པར་འཇུག་པ་ནི། འབྱིང་པར་འགྱུར།
འཇིབ་པར་འགྱུར། གཞུག་པར་འགྱུར། འཐོབ་པར་འགྱུར། འཆད་པར་
འགྱུར། ལྟ་བུ་དང༌། དེས་མཚོན་ནས་མོ་གཉིས་དང་མ་ཉིད་གསུམ་ལ་ཡང་
ཤེས་པར་བྱའོ། མིང་རྐྱང་ཙམ་ནི། གདུགས། སྟོབས། བདག
གཡབ། ཆོད། དུས། ལྟ་བུ་དང༌། ཞུགས་ཤིག །སྒྲུབས་ཤིག
ལྟ་བུ་བསྐུལ་ཚིག་དང༌། དེ་ལྟར་སྟོན་འཇུག་ལ་ལྟོས་པ་གཙོ་བོར་གསུངས་པའི་ཞར་

ལ་སྦྱོར་འཇུག་མེད་ཀྱང་གོང་བཞིན་བདག་གཞན་སོགས་སྟོན་ནུས་པའང་ཤེས་དགོས་པ་ནི། རྟོགས་བྱེད། རྟོགས་ཟིན། རྩོམ་བྱེད། གླིང་བྲ། སྐོར་བཞིན་པ། སྟོན་པར་འགྱུར། སྐྱོབས་ཤིག བྱས། ལྟ་བུ་དང་། ད་སའི་ཡང་འཇུག་གིས་འདས་པ་རང་དབང་དུ་སྟོན་པ། དཔེར་ན། གྱུར་ད། འདས། བྱས། གྲགས། ལྟ་བུའོ། །དེ་ལྟར་སའི་འཇུག་གསུམ་གྱིས་འདས་པ་དང་། འ་མཐའ་འདས་པ་ལ་གཏན་ནས་མི་འཇུག་པའི་ཁྱད་པར་ཙམ་ལས་གཞན་མ་འཇུག་ཡུལ་བདག་གཞན་སོགས་གང་ཡིན་ཚིག་གྲོགས་ཀྱིས་བསྒྱུར་བའི་ནུས་པར་ཤེས་དགོས་པ་ཡིན་ནོ། གཉིས་པ། ཕྱི་མ་ཇི་ལྟར་འགྱུར་བ་ནི། །ཞེས་པ། ཕྱི་མ་དག་གི་མིང་མཐའ་ཇི་ལྟར་འགྱུར་བ་རྣམ་དབྱེ་སོ་སོའི་ཐོབ་ཐང་ལ་དབྱེ་ན་བཞི་ལས་དང་པོ་ནི། རྗེས་འཇུག་པོ་ཡིས་པོ་ཡིག་གི །མིང་མཐའ་གཞན་དྲང་། །ཞེས་པ། མིང་སྔ་མའི་མཐའི་རྗེས་འཇུག་རྟགས་གསུམ་གང་ཡིན་པ་དེའི་མིང་དེ་ཉིད་ཀྱི་ཆ་ནས་མཐར་སྦྱོར་དགོས་པའི་མིང་མཐའ་ཡིན་ན་རྟགས་མཐུན་པར་འདྲེན་པ་ཤས་ཆེ་བས་རྗེས་འཇུག་པོས་མིང་གཞི་པོའི་མིང་མཐའ་འདྲེན་པ། དཔེར་ན། རྟོག་པ། དཔྱིད་ཀ ཐད་ཀ གཉིས་ཀ མཁྱེན་དཔ། འཁྱོར་དཔ། དགོངས་པ། ལྟ་བུ། གཉིས་པ། མོ་ཡིས་མོ་ཡི་མིང་མཐའ་དྲང་། །ཞེས་པ། གོང་དུ་རྗེས་འཇུག་པོས་པོའི་མིང་མཐའ་དྲངས་པ་དེ་བཞིན་དུ་མོ་ཡིས་མོའི་མིང་མཐའ་དྲང་བར་བྱ་སྟེ། དཔེར་ན། གསིང་མ། ཐམ་ག སླིང་ག དགའ་བ། ལྟ་བུ་དང་། གསུམ་པ། མ་ནིང་གིས་ནི་མ་ནིང་དྲང་། །ཞེས་པ། རྗེས་འཇུག་མ་ནིང་གིས་མིང་གཞི་མ་ནིང་དྲང་བར་བྱ་སྟེ། དཔེར་ན། དཀྱུན་཈། དབྱར་཈། སྤྱར་཈། འཕལ་཈། གསལ་཈། ལྟ་བུ་དང་། དེ་རྣམས་རྟགས་མཚུངས་འདྲེན་ཚུལ་ཏེ། །ཞེས་པ། གོང་གི་དེ་རྣམས་རྗེས་འཇུག་གི་རྟགས་དང་མིང་གཞིའི་རྟགས་རྟགས་མཚུངས་པར་འདྲེན་ཚུལ་ཡིན་ཏེ། ཞེས་པའོ། བཞི་པ། བརྗོད་བདེ་འདྲེན་པའང་ཤིན་ཏུ་མང་། །ཞེས་པ། གཙོ་ཆེ་བ་རྣམས་མིང་མཐའ་དང་མཐུན་པར་འདྲེན་ཚུལ་དེ་ལྟར་ཡིན་ཞིང་། །དེ་བྱིངས་བརྗོད་པ་བདེ་བའི་ཆེད་

དང་། འཇིག་རྟེན་པའི་ཉེར་སྤྱོད་དང་བསྟུན་དགོས་པ་སོགས་ཀྱིས་འདྲེན་ཚུལ་ཡང་ཤིན་ཏུ་མང་བར་འབྱུང་སྟེ་དེ་རྣམས་ཀྱང་བྱེ་བྲག་མ་འཛིངས་པར་རྟོགས་པར་བྱ་དགོས་ཏེ། དཔེར་ན། ཕོས་མོ་དྲངས་པ། ཐོག་མ། ལྟ་བུ་དང་། མོས་ཕོ་དྲངས་པ། ཁང་པ། ལྟ་བུ་དང་། མ་ནིང་གིས་མོ་དྲངས་པ། ཐལ་མོ། ལྟ་བུ་དང་། མ་ནིང་གིས་ཕོ་དྲངས་པ། ཆར་པ། ལྟ་བུ་མང་དུ་བྱུང་བ་ཤེས་དགོས་པར་མ་ཟད། གཞན་ཡང་བརྡ་རྙིང་ལ་རྟགས་མཚུངས་འདྲེན་པ་ཤིན་ཏུ་མང་ཡང་སྐད་གསར་བཅད་ཀྱི་ཞུ་དག་མང་བས་ནུབ་ཚུལ་གསུངས་པ་ལྟར་དཔེར་ན། བརྡ་རྙིང་རྟགས་མཚུངས་དྲངས་པ་ནི། བྲག་ཅ། དཀོན་ཅོག་རིན་ཅེན། ལྟ་བུ་ལ་བརྡ་གསར་ནི། བྲག་ཆ། དཀོན་མཆོག་རིན་ཆེན། ཞེས་པ་འདི་རྣམས་ཀྱང་རྟོགས་དགོས་པའི་གནད་དོ། །བརྗོད་བདེ་འདྲེན་ཚུལ་རྣམས་རྟགས་མ་མཐུན་ཀྱང་བརྗོད་བདེ་གཙོ་བོར་བྱས་ནས་སྒྲ་མཐུན་དྲངས་པ་ཡིན་པས་སུམ་རྟགས་གཉིས་ཀའི་དངོས་བསྟན་གྱི་དགོངས་པར་གནས་སོ། །གཞན་ཡང་མིང་མཐའ་དེ་ཉིད་ཀྱི། །རྟགས་མཚུངས་པའམ་སྒྲ་མཐུན་པའི། །རྣམ་དབྱེ་བརྒྱད་དང་སླར་བསྡུ་སོགས། །སྔ་མའི་ཤུགས་དང་མཐུན་པར་འདྲེན། །ཞེས་པ། གོང་གི་མིང་མཐའ་འདྲེན་ཚུལ་སོགས་བཤད་ཟིན་པ་དེ་ལས། གཞན་ཡང་རྣམ་དབྱེ་དང་དེ་མིང་ཚིག་ཕྲད་འདྲེན་ཚུལ་ནི། བཤད་མ་ཐག་པའི་མིང་མཐའ་དེ་ཉིད་ཀྱི་སྔ་མའི་རྗེས་འཇུག་གི་ཤུགས་ཀྱིས་རྣམ་དབྱེ་སོགས་རྟགས་པན་ཚུན་མཚུངས་པའམ་བརྗོད་བདེའི་སྒྲ་མཐུན་པའི་རྣམ་དབྱེ་དང་པོ་ཆོས་རྣམས་ངོ་བོ་ཙམ་བརྗོད་པ། གཉིས་པ་ལས་སུ་བྱ་བ། གསུམ་པ་བྱེད་སྒྲ། བཞི་པ་དགོས་ཆེད། ལྔ་པ་འབྱུང་ཁུངས། དྲུག་པ་འབྲེལ་སྒྲ། བདུན་པ་རྟེན་གནས། བརྒྱད་པ་བོད་པའི་སྒྲ་བཅས་བརྒྱད་དང་། དངོས་སུ་བསྟན་པ་སླར་བསྡུ། སོགས་ཁོངས་ནས་ཐོན་པ་ལྷག་བཅས། འབྱེད་སྡུད། བསྣན་པ། བདག་སྒྲ། ཚིག་རྒྱན། ཚེ་སྐབས་སོགས་ཀྱང་མིང་སྔ་མའི་ཤུགས་དང་མཐུན་པ་ཕྱི་མ་འདྲེན་དགོས་སོ་ཞེས་པའོ། །དེ་དག་ནང་གསེས་གང་འཇུག་ནི། །རྣམ་དབྱེའམ་འཕྲད་བཅས་མིང་ཚིག་དེའི། །མཐར་སྦྱར་མིང་དོན་

ལས་ཤེས་བྱ། །ཞེས་པ། བཤད་མ་ཐག་པ་དེ་དག་ནང་གསེས་གང་ལ་གང་
འཇུག་པ་ནི། རྣམ་དབྱེའམ་དེ་མིན་ཚིག་ཕྲད་བཅས་མིང་ཚིག་རྣམས་དེའི་མཐར་
སྦྱར་རྒྱུའི་མིང་དོན་འོག་མ་ལས་ལེགས་པར་ཤེས་པར་བྱའོ་ཞེས་པའོ། །དེ་ཡང་
ཆོས་རྣམས་ངོ་བོ་ཙམ། །བརྗོད་པ་རྣམ་དབྱེ་དང་པོ་སྟེ། །དཔེར་ན་བུམ་པ་ཀ་བ
བཞིན། །གསལ་བྱེད་བོད་ཀྱི་སྐད་ལ་ཙུང་། །ཞེས་པ། བཤད་མ་ཐག་པ་དེ་
ཡང་ཆོས་རྣམས་ཀྱི་ངོ་བོ་ཙམ་བརྗོད་པ་རྣམ་དབྱེ་དང་པོ་ཡིན་ལ་དེའི་གསལ་བྱེད་ནི།
དཔེར་ན། བུམ་པ། ཀ་བ། ལྷ། ལྷ་བུ་ངོ་བོ་ཙམ་བརྗོད་པ་ཉིད་དག་རྣམས་
སོགས་ཡིན་ཡང་བོད་ཁ་བ་ཅན་པ་རྣམས་ཀྱི་སྐད་ལ་ཤིན་ཏུ་ཙུང་ངོ་། །ཞེས་
པའོ། །ལས་དང་བྱ་ཡུལ་དོན་གཅིག་སྟེ། །དེ་ལྷའི་བྱ་བའི་ཡུལ་ཞིག་ལ། །བྱ་
བ་བྱས་པར་སྟོན་པ་ལ། །གཉིས་པ་ལས་སུ་བྱ་བ་དང་། །གཉིས་པའི་ནང་ཚན་དེ་
ཉིད་དང་། །བཞི་པ་དགོས་ཆེད་གསུམ་འདྲ་ཡང་། །བྱ་བ་བྱས་པས་བྱ་བའི་
ཡུལ། །དེ་འམ་དེ་དང་འབྲེལ་པ་ལ། །ཕན་ཐོགས་མེད་ན་གཉིས་པ་སྟེ། །
དཔེར་ན་ཤར་དུ་འགྲོ་ལྷ་བུ། །ཞེས་པ། ལས་དང་བྱ་བའི་ཡུལ་དོན་གཅིག་སྟེ་དེ་
ལྷ་བུའི་སྒོ་ནས་བྱ་བའི་ཡུལ་ཞིག་ལ་བྱ་བ་བྱས་པར་སྟོན་པ་དེ་ལ་རྣམ་དབྱེ་གཉིས་པ་ལས་
སུ་བྱ་བ་དང་། གཉིས་པའི་ནང་ཚན་དེ་ཉིད་དང་། བཞི་པ་དགོས་ཆེད་གསུམ་
འདྲ་བར་སྣང་མོད། དེ་རྣམས་ཀྱི་དབྱེ་བ་གང་གིས་འབྱེད་ན་བྱ་བ་བྱས་པས་བྱ་བའི་
ཡུལ་དེའམ་དེ་དང་འབྲལ་བ་ལ་ཕན་ཐོགས་མེད་ན་རྣམ་དབྱེ་གཉིས་པ་ལས་སུ་བྱ་བ་ཡིན་
ཏེ། དཔེར་ན། ཤར་དུ་འགྲོ། ལྷ་བུའོ། །ཕན་ཐོགས་ཡོད་ན་བཞི་པ་
སྟེ། །དཔེར་ན་སློང་ལ་སྦྱིན་ལྷ་བུ། །ཞེས་པ། བྱ་བ་བྱས་པས་བྱ་བའི་ཡུལ་
དེའམ་དེ་དང་འབྲེལ་བའི་ལས་ལ་ཕན་ཐོགས་ཡོད་ན་རྣམ་དབྱེ་བཞི་པ་དགོས་ཆེད་ཡིན་
ཏེ། དཔེར་ན། དགེ་སློང་ལ་སྦྱིན། སློང་མཁན་ལ་སྟེར། ཞིང་དུ་ཆུ་འདྲེན་
ལྷ་བུའོ། །ཕན་ཐོགས་མེད་ཀྱང་བྱ་ཡུལ་དང་། །བྱ་བ་ངོ་བོ་གཅིག་ཡིན་ན། །
གཉིས་པའི་ནང་ཚན་དེ་ཉིད་དེ། །དཔེར་ན་ལྷ་རུ་གསལ་ལྷ་བུ། །ཞེས་པ། བྱ་
བ་བྱས་པས་བྱ་བའི་ཡུལ་དེ་ལ་ཕན་ཐོགས་མེད་ཀྱང་བྱ་བའི་ཡུལ་དང་བྱ་བ་གཉིས་པོ་ངོ་

བོ་གཅིག་ཡིན་ན་རྣམ་དབྱེ་གཉིས་པའི་ནང་ཚན་དེ་ཉིད་ཡིན་ཏེ། །དཔེར་ན། ལྷ་རུ་གསལ། འོད་དུ་འཚེར། ལྟ་བུའོ། །གང་ཞིག་གང་ལ་བརྟེན་པའམ། །གནས་དང་ཡོད་པའི་དོན་ཙམ་ལས། །བྱ་བ་གཏན་ནས་མི་བྱེད་ན། །རྣམ་དབྱེ་བདུན་པ་གནས་གཞི་སྟེ། །དཔེར་ན་སྟེང་དུ་མི་ཡོད་ལྟར། །ཞེས་པ། ཆོས་གང་ཞིག་གཞི་གང་ལ་བརྟེན་པའམ་གནས་པའམ་ཡོད་པའི་དོན་སྟོན་པ་ཙམ་ལས་བྱ་བ་གཏན་ནས་མི་བྱེད་པ་ཡིན་ན་རྣམ་དབྱེ་བདུན་པ་གནས་གཞི་ཡིན་ཏེ། དཔེར་ན། སྟེང་དུ་མི་ཡོད། དབུས་སུ་ཇོ་བོ་བཞུགས། ལྟ་བུའོ། །ཚེ་སྐབས་གཉིས་དང་དོན་འདྲ་ན། །བདུན་པའི་ནང་ཚན་ཚེ་སྐབས་ཏེ། །དཔེར་ན་ཆུ་ཟླ་ཤར་པ་ན། །ཆོ་འཕྲུལ་དུས་ཆེན་ཚུགས་ལྟ་བུ། །ཞེས་པ། ཚེ་དང་སྐབས་གཉིས་ཀྱི་དོན་དང་འདྲ་ན་རྣམ་དབྱེ་བདུན་པའི་ནང་ཚན་ཚེ་སྐབས་ཡིན་ཏེ། དཔེར་ན། ཧོར་ཟླ་དང་པོ་ཤར་བ་ན་ཆོ་འཕྲུལ་དུས་ཆེན་ཚུགས། ལྟ་བུའོ། །རྣམ་དབྱེ་གཉིས་བཞི་བདུན་པ་དང་། དེ་ཉིད་ཚེ་སྐབས་གསལ་བྱེད་སྒྲ། །སུ་རུ་ར་དུ་ན་ལ་ཏུ། །ཡིན་ཞིང་ཕལ་ཆེར་ལ་སྒྲ་དང་། །མཐུན་པས་ལ་དོན་རྣམ་དབྱེའང་ཟེར། །ཞེས་པ། རྣམ་དབྱེ་གཉིས་པ། བཞི་པ། བདུན་པ། གཉིས་པའི་ནང་ཚན་དེ་ཉིད། བདུན་པའི་ནང་ཚན་ཚེ་སྐབས་བཅས་ལྔ་པོ་འདི་རྣམས་ཀྱི་དོན་གསལ་བར་བྱེད་པའི་སྒྲ་ནི། སུ་དང་། རུ་དང་། ར་དང་། དུ་དང་། ན་དང་། ལ་དང་། ཏུ་བཅས་བདུན་པོ་འདི་རྣམས་ཡིན་ཞིང་། ཕལ་ཆེར་ལ་སྒྲ་དང་འཇུག་ཚུལ་མཐུན་པས་ན་ལ་དོན་དང་། ཚིག་གྲོགས་ཀྱི་དབང་གིས་རྣམ་དབྱེར་གྱུར་ཚེ་ལ་དོན་གྱི་རྣམ་དབྱེའང་ཟེར་རོ། །འཇུག་ཚུལ་མཐུན་ལུགས་ནི། དབུས་སུ་འགྲོ། དབུས་ལ་འགྲོ། ལྟ་བུ་མཐུན་པས་སོ། །འོན་ཀྱང་ན་ལ་དེ་ཉིད་ལ། །མི་འཇུག་སྒྲ་བའི་སྒོ་ལས་གསུངས། །ཞེས་པ། འོན་ཀྱང་ན་ལ་གཉིས་ནི་རྣམ་དབྱེ་གཉིས་པའི་ནང་ཚན་དེ་ཉིད་ལ་མི་འཇུག་པ་སྒྲ་སྒོ་མཚོན་ཆ་ལས་གསུངས་ཏེ། སྒྲ་སྒོ་ལས། དུ་ལ་སོགས་པ་ལ་དང་མཐུན། །དེ་ཉིད་དག་ནི་ལྷག་པ་ཡིན། །གསུངས་སོ། འདིར་ཡང་ཕལ་ཆེར་ཞེས་མ་ངེས་པའི་ཚིག་སྨོས་པ་དཔེར་ན། ལྷ་ན་གསལ།

འོད་ལ་འཚོར། ལྟ་བུ་སྦྱར་མི་རུང་བའི་དོན་ཏོ། །རྣམ་དབྱེ་གང་ལ་སྦྱོར་ཡུལ་དེས། །ཉེ་འགྱུར་གང་དུ་བྱ་བ་ཞིག །བྱས་ན་གསུམ་པ་བྱེད་སྒྲ་སྟེ། །དཔེར་ན་བདག་གིས་བཤད་ལྟ་བུ། །ཞེས་པ། རྣམ་དབྱེ་གང་ལ་སྦྱོར་ཡུལ་དེས་ཉེ་བ་དང་འགྱུར་བ་གང་རིགས་སུ་བྱ་བ་ཞིག་བྱས་ན་རྣམ་དབྱེ་གསུམ་པ་བྱེད་སྒྲ་སྟེ། དཔེར་ན། བདག་གིས་བཤད། མིག་གིས་ལྟ་ལྟ་བུ་ཉེ་བ་དང་། མིག་གིས་ཤེལ་རྫེའི་རྫེ་མོ་ནས་ཕྱོགས་ཐམས་ཅད་དུ་ཡང་ཡང་དུ་ལེགས་པར་བལྟས་སོ། །ལྟ་བུ་འགྱུར་བའོ། །བྱ་བ་གཏན་ནས་མི་བྱེད་པར། །སྔ་ཕྱི་འབྲེལ་བྱེད་ཙམ་སྟོན་ན། །རྣམ་དབྱེ་དྲུག་པ་འབྲེལ་སྒྲ་སྟེ། །དཔེར་ན་བདག་གི་མིག་ལྟ་བུ། །ཞེས་པ། ལས་སམ་བྱ་བའི་ཡུལ་ལ་བྱ་བ་གཏན་ནས་མི་བྱེད་པར་ཚིག་སྔ་མ་དང་ཕྱི་མ་འབྲེལ་བྱེད་ཙམ་སྟོན་ན་རྣམ་དབྱེ་དྲུག་པ་འབྲེལ་སྒྲ་ཞེས་བྱ་སྟེ། དཔེར་ན། བདག་གི་མིག །ཁབ་ཀྱི་རྩེ། ལྟ་བུའོ། རྣམ་དབྱེ་དྲུག་གསུམ་གསལ་བྱེད་སྒྲ། །ས་མཐའ་ཡོད་དང་མེད་མ་ཡི། །གི་ཀྱི་གྱི་འི་ཡི་ལྔ་ཡིན། །ཞེས་པ། རྣམ་དབྱེ་དྲུག་པ་དང་གསུམ་པ་གཉིས་གསལ་བར་བྱེད་པའི་སྒྲ་ནི། ཚིག་གི་མཐའ་ན་ས་ཡོད་པ། གིས། ཀྱིས། གྱིས། འིས། ཡིས་དང་། ཚིག་གི་མཐའ་ན་ས་མེད་པ། གི། ཀྱི། གྱི། འི། ཡི་ལྔ་པོ་འདི་རྣམས་ཡིན་ནོ་ཞེས་པའོ། །གང་ཞིག་གང་ལས་འབྱུང་བའམ། །དབྱེ་དང་ལྟུང་བའི་དོན་ལྡན་ན། །རྣམ་དབྱེ་ལྔ་པ་འབྱུང་ཁུངས་ཏེ། །དཔེར་ན་ཞལ་ནས་ཐོས་ལྟ་བུ། །གསལ་བྱེད་སྒྲ་ནི་ནས་ལས་ཏེ། །དཀར་དང་སྡུད་པའང་ལྔ་པར་གཏོགས། །ཞེས་པ། ཆོས་གང་ཞིག་གཞི་གང་ལས་བྱུང་པའམ་བྱེ་བའམ་ལྟུང་བའི་དོན་དང་ལྡན་ན་རྣམ་དབྱེ་ལྔ་པ་འབྱུང་ཁུངས་ཞེས་བྱ་སྟེ། དཔེར་ན། ཞལ་ནས་ལེགས་བཤད་ཐོས། རྒྱ་མཚོ་ནས་ནོར་བུ་འབྱུང་ལྟ་བུ་དང་། དེ་རྣམས་གསལ་བྱེད་ཀྱི་སྒྲ་ནི་ནས་ལས་གཉིས་ཡིན་ཅིང་། དེར་མ་ཟད་དཀར་བ་དང་སྡུད་པ་གཉིས་ཀྱང་རྣམ་དབྱེ་ལྔ་པའི་ཁོངས་སུ་གཏོགས་ཏེ། དཔེར་ན། ལྷ་ཡི་ནང་ནས་བརྒྱ་སྦྱིན་མཆོག་ལྟ་བུ་དཀར་བ་དང་། སྤྱི་གཙུག་ནས་རྐང་མཐིལ་བར་ལྟ་བུ་སྡུད་པའོ། །གཞན་ཡང་ཚིག་དོན་གོང་འོག་ཏུ། །བསྡུ་རྒྱུ་

ཡོད་ན་སྤྱད་པའི་སྒྲ། དང་དང་ཀྱང་དང་ཡང་འང་སོགས་སྦྱོར། །ཞེས་པ།
གཞན་ཡང་ཚིག་གི་དོན་གོང་དང་འོག་གང་རིགས་སུ་བསྡུ་རྒྱུ་ཡོད་ན་སྤྱད་པའི་སྒྲ།
དང་དང་། ཀྱང་དང་། ཡང་དང་། འང་སོགས་སྦྱོར་དགོས་ཏེ། དཔེར་
ན། ལྷ་དང་མི་དང་ལྷ་མ་ཡིན་དང་དྲི་ཟར་བཅས་པའི་འཇིག་རྟེན་ཡི་རངས་ཏེ་ལྷ་བུ་
སྤྱད་པ་དང་། བསད་ཀྱང་ལངས། མགོ་ཡང་གུག་སྒྲ་འང་དཀར། ལྷ་
བུའོ། །རྣམ་གྲངས་དུ་མས་དོན་བསྒྱུར་ན། འཕྲེད་སྤྱད་སྒྲ་འཇུག །ཅེས་པ།
རྣམ་གྲངས་དུ་མས་དོན་བསྒྱུར་དགོས་ན་སྔ་མ་སྔ་མར་འཕྲེད་སྤྱད་ཀྱི་སྒྲ་འཇུག་སྟེ།
དཔེར་ན། དོན་བསྒྱུར་བ། འཆི་མེད་དམ། རྣམ་སད་དམ། མིག་མི་
འཛུམ་ནི་ལྷའོ། །ལྷ་བུ་དང་། ཚིག་བསྒྱུར་བ། པདྨ་དཀར་པོའམ། པདྨ་
དཀར་པོ་ལྷ་བུའི་སེམས་དཔའ། ལྷ་བུ་དང་། ཚིག་དོན་གཉིས་ཀ་བསྒྱུར་བ།
བསྐོར་ཞིང་བསྐོར་ཞིང་སླར་ཡང་དེ་རུ་འབབ། །ལྷ་བུའོ། །དགག་པ་དང་།
བདག་དོན་ཡོད་ན་ཐོག་མཐའ་རུ། །པ་སྡེའི་རྟགས་རྣམས་ཅི་རིགས་འཇུག །
ཅེས་པ། པ་སྡེའི་ཁོངས་ནས་བྱུང་བའི་མ་ཡིག་ཐོག་མཐའ་བར་གསུམ་གང་དུ་
ཞུགས་ཀྱང་དགག་པ་འམ་དགག་སྒྲ་ཡིན་ཏེ། མ་ཡིན། མི་འདུག བདག་
མེད། འདྲེ་མེད། མི་སྐྱུ་མ་ཡིན། གམ་ས། ལྷ་བུ་དང་། པ་སྡེའི་
ཁོངས་ནས་བྱུང་བའི་པ་དང་། མ་སྡེ་ཕོ་མོ་མ་ནིང་རྟགས་རྣམས་ཅི་
རིགས་སྦྱོན་པའི་བདག་སྒྲ་མིང་གཞིའི་མཐའ་རུ་ཞུགས་ན་བདག་པོའི་དོན་གསལ་བར་
བྱེད་པ་ཡིན་ཏེ། དཔེར་ན། རྟ་པ། ནང་པ། ལྷ་རྩེ་བ་ལྷ་བུའོ། རྒྱན་དུ་
གྱུར་པའི་ཚིག་ཕྲད་ཀྱང་། །དོན་ལ་བསྙེགས་ས་ཡོད་ན་སྦྱོར། །ཞེས་པ།
རྒྱན་དུ་གྱུར་པའི་ཚིག་གི་འཕྲད་རྣམས་ཀྱང་དོན་ལ་བསྙེགས་ས་སྟེ་སྦྱོར་ས་ཡོད་ན་སྦྱོར་
དགོས་ཏེ། དཔེར་ན། མཛེས་ཀྱང་མཛེས། བཏུད་ཀྱང་ཁྲོ་ལྷ་བུ་དང་། མི་
དགོས་པར་སྦྱོར་མི་རིགས་སོ། །དེ་བཞིན་བསྟན་བྱ་ལྷག་ཡོད་ན། །ལྷག་བཅས་
སྒྲ་སྦྱོར། །ཞེས་པ། བཤད་མ་ཐག་པའི་ཚིག་རྒྱན་གྱི་སྦྱོར་ཚུལ་དེ་བཞིན་དུ་
བསྟན་བྱ་ལྷག་མ་ཡོད་ན་ལྷག་བཅས་ཀྱི་སྒྲ་སྦྱོར་དགོས་ཏེ། དཔེར་ན། དོན་

རྟོགས་ཏེ་ཉམས་སུ་བླངས། ལྷ་བུའོ། །ཚིག་དོན་ནི། །རྫོགས་ན་སླར་བསྡུའི་སྒྲ་རྣམས་སྦྱོར། །ཞེས་པ། གང་བརྗོད་རྒྱུའི་ཚིག་དོན་ནི་རྫོགས་ན་སླར་བསྡུའི་སྒྲ་རྣམས་སྦྱོར་དགོས་ཏེ། དཔེར་ན། མཆོག་གོ བཟང་ངོ་། ལྷ་བུའོ། །

རྗེས་འཇུག་གི་དགོས་པ་བསྟན་པ་ནི། །དགོས་པ་ཅི་ཕྱིར་འཇུག་ཅེ་ན། །མོ་ཡིག་དབྱངས་དང་མི་ལྡན་ན། །ཕོ་ཡིག་གསལ་བྱེད་བརྗོད་མི་ནུས། །ཞེས་པ། རྗེས་འཇུག་གི་ཡི་གེ་རྣམས་དགོས་པ་ཅི་ཕྱིར་འཇུག་པར་བྱེད་ཅེ་ན། མོའི་ཡི་གེ་དབྱངས་ཡིག་རྣམས་དང་མི་ལྡན་ན། ཕོ་ཡིག་གསལ་བྱེད་རྣམས་བརྗོད་མི་ནུས་པ་ཡིན་ནོ་ཞེས་པའོ། །དེ་ཕྱིར་དབྱངས་ལྷར་བཞེད་པ་བདེ། །ཕོ་ཡིག་དབྱངས་ལྡན་དེ་དག་ལའང་། །རྗེས་འཇུག་བཅུ་པོ་མ་ཞུགས་ན། །དོན་གྱི་ངོ་བོ་ཙམ་སྟོན་པའི། །མིང་དང་དོན་གྱི་ཁྱད་པར་རྣམས། །སྟོན་པའི་ཚིག་དང་དོན་ལྡན་པའི། །ངག་གི་བརྗོད་པ་ཡོད་མིན་ཏེ། །ཡི་གེའི་ཁོངས་ནས་མིང་དབྱུང་ཞིང་། །མིང་གི་ཁོངས་ནས་ཚིག་ཕྱུང་ནས། །ཚིག་གིས་དོན་རྣམས་སྟོན་པས་སོ། །ཞེས་པ། རྒྱུ་མཚན་དེའི་ཕྱིར་དབྱངས་ཡིག་དངོས་བསྟན་བཞི་དང་ཤུགས་བསྟན་ཨ་བཅས་ལྷར་བཞེད་པ་བདེ་བར་མ་ཟད་ཕོའི་ཡི་གེ་ཀ་སོགས་ལ་དབྱངས་སམ་གི་གུ་སོགས་དང་ལྡན་པ་དེ་དག་ལའང་རྗེས་འཇུག་གི་ཡི་གེ་བཅུ་པོ་གང་རུང་ཞིག་མ་ཞུགས་ན་དོན་གྱི་ངོ་བོ་སྟོན་པའི་མིང་དང་། །དོན་གྱི་ཁྱད་པར་སྟོན་པའི་ཚིག་དང་། བརྗོད་བྱའི་དོན་དང་ལྡན་པའི་ངག་གི་བརྗོད་པ་གང་ཡང་ཡོད་མིན་ཏེ། ཡི་གེའི་ཁོངས་སམ་ནང་ནས་མིང་དབྱུང་བ་སྐྱེ་བྱུང་ཞིང་། མིང་གི་ཁོངས་ནས་ཚིག་རྣམས་ཕྱུང་ནས་ཚིག་གིས་དོན་རྣམས་མ་འདྲེས་པར་སོ་སོར་སྟོན་པར་ནུས་པས་སོ་ཞེས་པའོ། །མིང་ཚིག་བརྗོད་པ་མེད་ན་ནི། །ཐུན་མོང་ཐུན་མོང་མ་ཡིན་པའི། །ཤེས་བྱ་སྟོན་པའང་མེད་པར་འགྱུར། །ཞེས་པ། མིང་དང་ཚིག་གི་བརྗོད་པ་མེད་ན་ནི་ཕྱི་རོལ་པ་དང་ཐུན་མོང་པའི་སྐད་དངགས་ལ་སོགས་པའི་རིག་བྱེད་རྣམས་དང་། ཐུན་མོང་མ་ཡིན་པ་ཐུབ་པ་སངས་རྒྱས་བཅོམ་ལྡན་འདས་ཀྱིས་གསུངས་པའི་མདོ་སྔགས་ཀྱི་བཀའ་བསྟན་བཅོས་རྣམས་ཀྱི་གཞུང་དོན་ལ་ཤེས་པར་བྱ་བའི་ཡུལ་སྟོན་

པའང་མེད་པར་འགྱུར་རོ། །ཞེས་པའོ། །དེ་ཕྱིར་འཕགས་ཡུལ་མཁས་རྣམས་ཀྱི། །རྗེས་སུ་འབྲང་ནས་གསུངས་པ་འདི། །སྐྱེ་བོ་ཀུན་གྱིས་རྟོགས་གྱུར་ཅིག །ཅེས་པ། དགོས་པ་དེའི་ཕྱིར་ན་རྒྱ་གར་འཕགས་ཡུལ་དུ་བྱོན་པའི་མཁས་པ་ཆེན་པོ་བྲམ་ཟེ་ལི་བི་ཀ་ར་ལ་སོགས་པ་རྣམས་ཀྱི་རྗེས་སུ་འབྲངས་ནས་ཐོན་མི་ཉིད་ཀྱི་བརྩེ་བས་ཀུན་ནས་བསླངས་ཏེ་གསུངས་པའི་བསྟན་བཅོས་སུམ་བཅུ་པ་དང་རྟགས་ཀྱི་འཇུག་པ་འདི་གཉིས་ཀྱི་དགོངས་དོན་རྣམས་ཕྱིན་ཅི་མ་ལོག་པར་གངས་ཅན་གྱི་སྐྱེ་བོ་ཀུན་གྱིས་བདེ་བླག་ཏུ་རྟོགས་པར་གྱུར་ཅིག །ཅེས་ཐུགས་སྨོན་མཛད་པའོ། ། ཚིག་གི་སྒྲ་ཙམ་འདྲ་ན་ཡང་། །དོན་ལ་ཁྱད་པར་ཤིན་ཏུ་ཆེ། །དེ་ཕྱིར་བརྡ་དག་ལ་བརྟེན་ནས། །མ་ནོར་དོན་རྣམས་འཚོལ་བ་གཅེས། །ཞེས་པ། མིང་ཕན་ཚུན་ཚིག་གི་སྒྲ་ཙམ་འདྲ་བར་སྣང་ཡང་དོན་ལ་ཁྱད་པར་ཤིན་ཏུ་ཆེ་བ་ཡོད་དེ། དཔེར་ན། གྲི་ལྟ་བུར་མཚོན་ན། ག་གྲི། ད་དྲི། བ་བྲི། སོགས་ཕན་ཚུན་མིང་གཞིའི་སྒྲ་ཙམ་འདྲ་ན་ཡང་སོ་སོར་འབྱེད་ན་མཚོན་གྱི་རལ་གྲི་ལ་ག་གྲི། སྣ་ལ་བསྣམ་བྱའི་དྲི་ལ་ད་དྲི། རི་མོ་བྲི་ལ་བ་བྲི་སོགས་ཁྱད་པར་ཤིན་ཏུ་ཆེ་སྟེ། དེ་ཡང་སྔོན་རྒྱལ་པོ་ལྷང་དང་། གུང་གཉིས་ཀྱང་མི་མཐུན་པའི་གཞི་ཡི་གེ་འདྲི་བ་པོས་ད་དྲིག་གྲི་ནོར་འཁྲུལ་བྱུང་རྐྱེན་གྱིས་འཐབ་རྩོད་བྱུང་བའི་ལོ་རྒྱུས་ཀྱང་གསུངས་སོ། །རྒྱུ་མཚན་དེའི་ཕྱིར་བཤེས་གཉེན་དམ་པའི་ཞབས་པད་བསྟེན་ནས་བརྡ་དག་པར་བྱེད་པའི་བརྡ་སྤྲོད་ཀྱི་གཞུང་རྣམས་ལ་བརྟེན་ནས་སྦྱངས་སྟོབས་ཕུལ་ཕྱིན་གྱིས་མིང་ཚིག་རྣམས་ཀྱི་དབྱེ་བ་མ་ནོར་བར་བྱས་ནས་དོན་རྣམས་འཚོལ་བ་སྙིང་གི་དབུས་སུ་གཅེས་པར་བཟུང་དགོས་སོ། །ཞེས་པའོ། །དོན་ལ་མི་རྨོངས་རྨོངས་པ་ཡང་། །ལུགས་འདིར་མཁས་མིན་གྱིས་བྱེད་དེ། །སྒྲ་ཤེས་དོན་ལ་མི་རྨོངས་ཞེས། །མཁས་པའི་གསུང་ལ་ཡོངས་སུ་གྲགས། །ཞེས་པ། དེ་ལྟར་བརྡ་དག་གི་གཞུང་ལ་ཐོས་བསམ་གྱི་སྒོ་ནས་ཞུགས་ན་རྒྱལ་བའི་གསུང་རབ་དང་དགོངས་འགྲེལ་རྒྱ་བོད་མཁས་གྲུབ་ཀྱི་གཞུང་དོན་རྣམས་ཀྱི་དགོངས་པ་འབྱེད་པ་ལ་མི་རྨོངས་པའི་བློ་གྲོས་མཆོག་ཏུ་རྒྱས་ནས་མཁས་པ་ཆེན་པོར་འགྱུར་ཞིང་། བརྡ་དག་གཞུང་ལ་ཐོས་བསམ་གྱིས་མ་ཞུགས་ན

བཀའ་དང་དགོངས་འགྲེལ་མ་ཟད་ཐ་ན་སྲིད་ཀྱི་བྱ་བཞག་གི་དོན་ལའང་མི་ཤེས་པའི་
རྨོངས་པར་འགྱུར་བ་སྟེ། དེ་ལྟར་རྨོངས་མི་རྨོངས་ཀྱང་རྩ་བ་བརྡ་སྤྲོད་ཀྱི་གཞུང་
སུམ་རྟགས་གཉིས་པོ་འདིར་མཁས་མི་མཁས་ཀྱིས་བྱེད་དེ་བོད་དུ་སྒྲ་སུམ་རྟགས་ཡིན་
ཞིང་སྒྲ་ཤེས་ན་དོན་ལ་མི་རྨོངས་ཞེས་རྒྱ་བོད་ཀྱི་མཁས་གྲུབ་རྣམས་ཀྱི་གསུང་ལ་ཡང་
ཡོངས་སུ་གྲགས་པ་ཡིན་ནོ་ཞེས་པའོ། །འདི་ལ་མ་སྦྱངས་རྨོངས་ཚོད་ཀྱིས། །
འཆད་རྩོད་རྩོམ་པའི་གྲྭར་འཛུག་པ། །ཨ་སྐྱེས་སེང་ལྤགས་གྱོན་པ་བཞིན། །ནམ་
ཞིག་རྗེས་ངན་གསལ་བར་འགྱུར། །ཞེས་པ། བརྡ་དག་གི་གཞུང་ལུགས་ཀུན་གྱི་
མ་ཕྱིར་གྱུར་པ་སུམ་རྟགས་འདི་ལ་མ་སྦྱངས་པ་འམ་མ་བསླབ་པར་རྨོངས་ཚོགས་སྤྱི་
བརྗོལ་གྱིས་རྒྱལ་བའི་གསུང་རབ་ཀྱི་དགོངས་དོན་གཞན་ལ་འཆད་པ་དང་། ཕ་རོལ་
པོ་དང་རྩོད་པ་བྱེད་པ་དང་། རང་གིས་རྩོམ་པ་སོགས་མཁས་པའི་བྱ་བ་གསུམ་གྱི་
གྲྭར་རམ་གྲས་སུ་འཛུག་པར་བྱེད་པ་དེ་ནི། དཔེར་ན་ཨ་སྐྱེས་སེང་གེའི་པགས་པ་
གྱོན་པ་དེ་གནས་སྐབས་སེངྒེ་ལྟ་བུར་མངོན་ནའང་དུས་ནམ་ཞིག་གི་ཚེ་ཨའི་གཟུགས་
བརྙན་གསལ་བར་མཐོང་བའི་རྗེས་ངན་སྟོན་པ་དེ་བཞིན་དུ་སྐབས་དེར་འཆད་རྩོད་
སོགས་གྲྭར་ཞུགས་ཀྱང་ནམ་ཞིག་མ་སྦྱངས་པའི་རྗེས་ངན་རྣམས་གསལ་བར་སྟོན་པར་
འགྱུར་རོ་ཞེས་པའོ། །དེ་ཕྱིར་བློ་གསལ་དོན་གཉེར་རྣམས། །རྟགས་འཇུག་
དཀའ་གནད་གཟུགས་བརྙན་ཀུན། །གསལ་བར་འཆར་བའི་མེ་ལོང་འདིར། །
ལ་ཟུར་གཟིགས་མོར་སྤྱོན་དང་ཀྱེ། །ཞེས་པ། རྒྱུ་མཚན་དེའི་ཕྱིར་བློ་གསལ་
ཐོས་བསམ་གྱི་དོན་གཉེར་དང་ལྡན་པ་རྣམས་རྟགས་འཇུག་གི་དཀའ་གནད་དམ་དོན་
རྟོགས་དཀའ་ཞིང་གནད་ཆེ་བ་རྣམས་ཀྱི་གཟུགས་བརྙན་ཀུན་མ་འདྲེས་པར་གསལ་བར་
འཆར་བའི་མེ་ལོང་འདི་ཉིད་ཀྱི་ངོས་ལ་ལ་ཟུར་ཏེ་མགྱོགས་པར་གཟིགས་མོ་འམ་ལྟད་
མོ་ལྟ་བར་སྤྱོན་དང་ཀྱེ་ཞེས་བོས་པ་ནི་ད་ལྟ་འདིར་བྱོན་ཅིག་བློ་གསལ་རྣམས། ཞེས་
པའོ། །འདི་ལ་ནོངས་པའི་ཚོགས་མཆིས་ན། །གཟུར་གནས་མཁས་པའི་སྤྱན་
སྔར་འཆགས། །ཞེས་པ། རྟགས་འཇུག་དཀའ་གནད་གསལ་བའི་མེ་ལོང་འདི་
ལ་ནོར་འཁྲུལ་གྱི་ནོངས་པ་སྟེ་ཉེས་པའི་ཚོགས་མཆིས་ན། གཟུར་གནས་སམ་དྲང་

པོར་གནས་པའི་མཁས་པ་ཀུན་གྱི་ན་སྔར་འགྲོལ་ལོ་འཆགས་སམ་བཤགས་སོ། །
ཞེས་པའོ། །ཅུང་ཟད་འབད་ལས་ཐོབ་པའི་དགེས། །ཀུན་གྱིས་འདི་དོན་རྟོགས་
པར་ཤོག །ཅེས་པ། དབྱངས་ཅན་གྲུབ་པའི་རྡོ་རྗེ་བདག་གིས་རྟགས་འཇུག་གི་
གཞུང་འདི་ཉིད་བསྐྲུན་པའི་ངལ་བ་ཅུང་ཟད་འབད་ལས་ཐོབ་པའི་དགེ་བ་དེས་གངས་
ཅན་འགྲོ་བ་ཀུན་གྱིས་འདིའི་དོན་ལེགས་པར་རྟོགས་ནས་འཆད་རྩོད་རྩོམ་གསུམ་ལ་
སོགས་པའི་སྒོ་ནས་རང་གཞན་གྱི་དོན་རྣམས་མཐར་ཕྱིན་པར་བྱེད་ནུས་པར་ཤོག་
ཅིག །ཅེས་བསྔོ་སྨོན་མཛད་དོ། །འདིར་སྨྲས་པ། ཐུ་མིའི་ཐུགས་བསྐྱེད་ཆུ་
གཏེར་བསྲུབས་པ་ལས། །འོངས་པའི་སུམ་རྟགས་དགོས་འདོད་ནོར་གྱི་
དབྱིག །ཕན་བདེའི་འོད་འབར་སྣང་བའི་དཔལ་ཡོན་ཅན། །འདི་ཀོ་སྔོན་བྱོན་
མཁས་རྣམས་མིག་བཞིན་གཅེས། །དེ་ཕྱིར་གཞུང་འགྲེལ་ནམ་མཁའི་སྐར་ཚོགས་
བཞིན། །རང་རང་ཕྲེང་སོའི་འཕྲོ་འདུ་མཁས་པའི་དབུས། །སྐལ་བཟང་ཀུནྡའི་
འཛུམ་པ་ལྷུག་པོ་རུ། །འགྲོལ་ནུས་དངུལ་ཆུའི་ལེགས་བཤད་ཟླ་སྣང་མཆོག །
ཨེ་མ་བཟང་དག་གཞུང་ལུགས་རྒྱ་མཚོའི་མཐའ། །བྱིས་བློའི་མིག་གི་སྤྱོད་ཡུལ་ག་
ལ་ཞག །དེ་སྐད་འདི་ལ་ནོངས་པའི་ཚོགས་མཆིས་ན། །གཟུར་གནས་མཁས་
ལ་འཆགས་སོ་བྱི་དོར་མཛོད། །ཅུང་ཟད་འབད་ལས་ཐོབ་པའི་དགེ་བའི་ཆ། །ཁ་
བ་དུང་དང་པད་རྩ་འོ་མཚོ་ལྟར། །དཀར་བ་གང་དེས་ལུང་རྟོགས་དམ་པའི་
ཆོས། །རང་གཞན་རྒྱུད་ལ་མཆོག་ཏུ་རྒྱས་གྱུར་ཅིག །ཅེས་པ་འདི་ཡང་རང་
སློབ་རྩེ་དྲུང་རྒྱལ་མཚན་ཆོས་ལྡན་ལགས་ཀྱིས་རྟགས་འཇུག་དཀའ་གནད་གསལ་བའི་
མེ་ལོང་གི་འགྲེལ་པ་ཕལ་ཆེག་གོ་བདེ་བ་ཞིག་དགོས་ཞེས་ནན་གྱིས་བསྐུལ་བར།
རང་ངོས་ནས་འདི་ལྟར་སྨྲ་བའི་སྤོབས་པ་རྟུལ་ཕྲན་ཙམ་མ་མཆིས་ཀྱང་སྐུལ་བ་པོའི་
གསུང་ངོ་མ་ལྡོག་པར་སྤྲོ་བརྩོལ་བསྐྱེད་ནས་ཧྲི་ཀླུ་དཀའ་ཆེན་པདྨ་སྐྱེས་བུའི་དོན་གྲུབ་
འབྲས་བུ་ཟླ་བའི་དཀར་ཕྱོགས་རྫོགས་པ་གསུམ་པའི་ཉིན་མཇུག་གྲུབ་པར་བགྱིས་པའོ།།
||

Index

Ingram Content Group UK Ltd.
Milton Keynes UK
UKHW010712100423
419909UK00001B/134

9 789937 572286